GLOBAL HISTORY

GLOBAL HISTORY

A Short Overview

Noel Cowen

Polity

First published in 2001 by Polity Press in association with Blackwell Publishers Ltd

Editorial office:
Polity Press
65 Bridge Street
Cambridge CB2 1UR, UK

Marketing and production:
Blackwell Publishers Ltd
108 Cowley Road
Oxford OX4 1JF, UK

Published in the USA by
Blackwell Publishers Inc.
350 Main Street
Malden, MA 02148, USA

ISBN 0-7456-2805-2
ISBN 0-7456-2806-0 (pbk)

A catalogue record for this book is available from the British Library and has been applied for from the Library of Congress.

Typeset in 11 on 13 pt Sabon
by Best-set Typesetter Ltd., Hong Kong
Printed in Great Britain by MPG Books, Bodmin, Cornwall

This book is printed on acid-free paper.

Contents

Acknowledgements

My first and heartfelt acknowledgement is to my son Robin whose belief in this project has been constant for twenty-five years. From the international sixth-form Atlantic College in Wales he won a Fairbridge scholarship to the University of Western Australia to study philosophy, politics and history. Searching through the current literature on the philosophy of history, Robin felt bound to report: 'The central goal to afford a total explanatory account of the past is now very unsympathetically regarded.' But he added his opinion that my theory was 'eminently plausible'. His subsequent commitment was to the foundation of sound education in primary schools in Australia and England. But his interest in my plausible enterprise never wavered, and in correspondence and recorded discussion he injected something of the intellectual rigour of his M.A. thesis in philosophy into the narrative I was piecing together.

Born in the naval and military town of Chatham during one of the worst episodes of the Great War, as I grew to manhood I learned with mounting horror of the sheer wickedness of the Battle of the Somme. In my last years at school and as a young newspaper reporter I was increasingly aware of the new chapters of wickedness that threatened a return to global conflict. I registered as a conscientious objector at the onset of the Second World War, and in its aftermath I was recruited to a small team at the Ministry of Economic Affairs to help explain our economic plight. When

the Ministry was merged into the Treasury I worked on problems of reconstruction in an emerging global context. I learnt
about the stern economics of recurrent crisis and our dependence for survival on international political cooperation and
the definition of common goals for war-ravaged nations.
Stimulated by Toynbee's *A Study of History*, but unconvinced
by its core arguments, I sent him some criticisms and some
thoughts of my own. In his reply he said 'the more of us have
a go at it the better.'

With this encouragement I began an extensive programme
of reading which has never really ended. My plan was to
eschew theory for the time being and search the works of
specialist historians for detailed factual accounts of particular civilizations. My debt to them is enormous, not only for
the knowledge and insight they have given me but also for
the pleasures of wandering in their enchanted garden. The
City of Westminster library responded with zeal to my
growing lists of books, which they bought or borrowed when
they were not available on their shelves. I welcomed the
opportunity to move to the Ministry of Education and to
profit, thereby, from the scholarly wisdom of H.M. Inspec-
tors, one of whom in particular was seeking to arouse an
interest in world history in the secondary schools. Teddy
(E. E. Y.) Hales had published a number of historical works
and was currently working on curricular ideas based on discussions with international educationists. We discussed the
relevance of this background to my studies.

In an article I published around that time I first spelt out
the global dimensions of my work, referring to 'the global
view' which was discernible in 'the unfolding of the regional
sequences'. After discussing 'the ends pursued in turn by man
the wanderer, man the settler, man the conqueror and man
the worshipper', I turned to 'the global situation' taking
shape and asked if there were any signs of a common direction emerging. In discussions with Robin I undertook several
reworkings of my material and in the 1980s I concluded a
comparative treatment of classical and modern civilizations
with a summary of increasing global trends against the back-

ground of technological and financial innovation. Drawing the strands together, I wrote that 'the essential conditions for a sustainable civilisation of global dimensions in the future would be, on the analogy of the past, the material means to sustain its population, a system of government to give security and stability, and a supportive ethos widely enough recognised and upheld.'

I had by then retired from government service and could spend more time on research, notably in Exeter University library and in the university library in Perth, Western Australia. Shortly afterwards I became aware of an explosion of interest in world history in the United States. I joined the ten-year-old World History Association, studied the Journal of World History, and visited the States to talk about my work. I was well received and in 1996 I was invited to address the final plenary session of the annual international WHA conference. Although illness prevented me from attending the conference, this American connection had several further consequences. The first was that I wrote an account of modern American civilization compared with modern Japanese civilization, showing correspondences between both and with the early modern and classical civi-lizations. The second consequence was an interest in what was becoming known as 'global history', which appeared to be the history of the concept of globalization. Applying this notion to my account of civilization I wrote a new shorter study entitled 'Civilisation and Globalisation'. The third consequence was that I attended the 1997 Anglo-American Conference of Historians on European Peoples and the Non-European World. Encouraged by the conference document, which called for guidelines and big pictures of world history, I sent a copy of the synopsis of my book to the organizer, Professor Patrick K. O'Brien, the retiring director of the London Institute of Historical Research. In his reply he thought I had 'lighted on two organising or ordering concepts'.

In 1999 I realized the relevance of my studies to what Pro-fessor David Held and his colleagues were describing as 'the globalization debate' and I sent a copy of my book to Polity Press. The prompt and positive response I received from David Held and the suggestions subsequently forthcoming from Polity readers resulted in substantial revisions and additions. The book now published is the product of half a century of study, welcomed by Toynbee in its early stages, supported by my son Robin throughout, and given recognition at the end by David Held and Polity. My wife Helen has been a sympathetic and long-suffering participant in this obsessive enterprise and to her this final outcome is gratefully dedicated.

The author and publishers would like to thank the following for permission to reproduce copyright material:

Cambridge University Press for the map on p. 128 from I.M. Lapidus, *A History of Islamic Societies* (1988), p. 243;

Gerald Duckworth and Co. Ltd for the map on p. 62 from N.G.L. Hammond, *The Genius of Alexander the Great* (1997), p. 126;

Octopus Publishing Group Ltd for the maps on pp. 98, 140 and 146 from *Philip's Atlas of World History*, pp. 44, 112, 115. Copyright © George Philip Ltd, 1999;

Oxford University Press, Inc. for the map on p. 84 from Jerry H. Bentley, *Old World Encounters: Cross-Cultural Contacts and Exchanges in Pre-Modern Times* (1993), p. 34. Copyright © 1993 Oxford University Press;

Random House Group Ltd for the map on p. 20 from C. Stringer and R. McKie, *African Exodus*, Pimlico (1996), p. 169;

Every effort has been made to trace all the copyright holders, but if any have been inadvertently overlooked the publishers will be pleased to make the necessary arrangement at the first opportunity.

Introduction

The time frame in which to locate the global history of mankind was effectively shown by two academic events which occurred in the late 1980s. In 1987 an international conference in Cambridge of specialists in human evolution, archaeology and molecular genetics found evidence that there were anatomically modern human beings 100,000 years ago. There was wide support for the view that, following an exodus from east Africa, their descendants went on to occupy all the continents of the Earth.[1] At about the same time a research project on the global forces now shaping our lives was being formulated in an application to the Economic and Social Research Council. The results have now been published in a book on global transformations in politics, economics and culture, which reaches the conclusion that globalization 'is an idea whose time has come'.[2] Between these two parameters, where are meaningful guidelines to be drawn?

The answer I believe lies in a significant shift in world history studies in the last quarter-century. Three strands in particular have come together, one from the study of civilizations, another from the concept of world-systems, and the third from the idea of global history. Together they map out a course across the millennia.

The leading exponent of the first strand is William H. McNeill, an early associate of Arnold J. Toynbee who in a famous study treated civilizations as separate but related entities.[3] After the appearance of the last of Toynbee's twelve volumes in 1961 McNeill set out to improve on him 'by showing how the separated civilisations of Eurasia interacted'.[4] Finally he concluded that 'a proper world history ought to focus primarily upon changes in the ecumenical world system, and then proceed to fit developments within separate civilisations ... into the pattern of that fluctuating whole.'[5] From McNeill, therefore, we have the idea that civilizations in themselves are a valid field of study, as well as the interactions between them.

This fitted well with a study of the modern world-system by Immanuel Wallerstein, the first volume of which had been published in 1974, arguing that world-economies were 'divided into core-states and peripheral areas'.[6] His particular concern was that in the sixteenth century 'there came into existence what we may call a world-economy.'[7] This proposition has led to a vigorous debate on whether such a system had a history of 5,000 years or was the latest in a series of world-systems, each with a changing structure. Implicit in this debate is the idea that regional interactions have gradually developed to the point where we can meaningfully talk about a global world system.

The third strand became visible in the late 1980s with discussions across a wide range of disciplines on what were being called 'global issues'. Among these forums was an international conference at Bellagio in Italy in 1991 and the publication in 1993 of a collection of essays linked by the idea of 'conceptualizing global history'.[8] In 1999 the concept was given detailed and authoritative treatment in the book mentioned above on global transformations in the contemporary era. Emphasizing the need to look beyond the modern era, to offer an explanation of a process 'which has a long history', this study called for an 'analytical framework offering a platform for contrasting and comparing different phases or historical forms'.[9]

Civilizations

The study of civilizations became very popular after the First World War in response to publications by Oswald Spengler in Germany, Arnold Toynbee in Britain and Pitirin Sorokin and others in America. Continuing up to the years of the Second World War, such works were a reaction against national histories, a reaction which had begun to appear in the second half of the nineteenth century. During that century the idea had been entertained that a science of history and society might be possible that was akin to the natural sciences. An international effort emerged to give status to the study of sociology, in which the parts of a society could be seen as cohering into a unity, an integrated system with a life character of its own.

Among those who explored this idea was the French scholar Émile Durkheim, who was deeply distressed by the war of 1870 with Germany and the consequences of defeat and social breakdown. He argued that society existed independently of particular individuals, maintaining itself like an organism. In Germany after the 1914 war Oswald Spengler applied this concept to large complexes of political, social, economic and cultural elements passing through cycles of birth, development and decay. He believed that western society was in irreversible decline. Sorokin, for his part, was expelled from Russia for opposing Bolshevism and founded the department of sociology at Harvard, where he wrote at length about the crisis of western society and about civilizations and cultures that in their balances of values and conditions had distinguishable life cycles of growth and decline. His four volumes of *Social and Cultural Dynamics* appeared between 1939 and 1941. Between 1934 and 1961 Toynbee published the twelve volumes of *A Study of History* in which he identified twenty-three civilizations, described their life cycles and looked for principles that governed their lives. While much of this elaborate edifice has ceased to command support, the study of civilizations has received a new lease of life in the contacts between them, including economic exchanges and technological and cultural borrowings.

World systems

By the 1970s, however, a new perspective on world history studies was emerging, with roots in the intense battles of the American student rebellion of the previous decade and a background in the revolutionary ideologies of what was being called the Third World. The projection of world social history offered by Immanuel Wallerstein in the first volume of *The Modern World-System* in 1974 appeared to respond to these influences with a comprehensive theory that made sense of actual world events. His strategy was to identify the social system in which capitalism had grown as a world economy, thus differing from political empires which were dominated by strong centres. This, he hoped, might end debates about the comparability of societies and the degree to which generalizations could be formed about them. He found it necessary to trace the history of the capitalist world economy from the sixteenth century, because that was when it began, believing that if societies went through stages so did the world system. Changes in sovereign states could then be explained as consequences of the evolution and interaction of the 'world-system'.

In 1989, when his third volume appeared, covering the second era of great expansion between 1730 and the 1840s, Janet Abu-Lughod published a book called *Before European Hegemony*. This argued that between 1250 and 1350 many parts of the Old World began to become integrated into a single system of exchange, and that an even earlier world system (excluding northern Europe) had existed some two thousand years ago. McNeill, however, writing a foreword to papers on the world system in 1993, gave the opinion that a market that embraced the whole world could only arise after 1500 with the arrival of global shipping.[10] The argument was already shifting towards a global history, with antecedents that included Wallerstein's system. It was perhaps no accident that in looking for an intellectual base Wallerstein had turned to Fernand Braudel, who had coined the phrase 'histoire globale'.

Global history

Braudel, who had shifted from civilizations to world systems, wrote of 'histoire globale' in the sense of there being no boundaries to the subject, and in 1972 he called for a history whose scope would extend to all the sciences of man, to the 'globality of the human sciences'. In his account of the Mediterranean world in the sixteenth century, and in his three-volume account of civilization and capitalism from the fifteenth to the eighteenth centuries, he combined a broad vision with a meticulous attention to detail. These immense works appeared between 1949 and 1979. They were limited to the premodern world, and primarily to economic history, but they had established the concept of thinking globally, which for him was 'the only form of history capable of satisfying us now'.

What this might mean remained uncertain, not least in the context of what were seen as Three Worlds (capitalist, communist and uncommitted), the subject of a would-be definitive account in 1984.[11] Five years later the Berlin Wall was pulled down, and in November 1990 the end of the Cold War was formally proclaimed. By the end of the century a different world was ten years old, as a new international system of global integration began to give substance to Braudel's vision. During that decade significant attempts were made 'to develop a more comprehensive explanation of globalization which highlights the complex intersection between a multiplicity of driving forces'.[12] In 1995 Michael Geyer and Charles Bright, writing about world history in a global era, argued that the central challenge at the end of the twentieth century was 'to narrate the world's past in an age of globality'. This would not 'refuse or jettison the findings of world-systems theories or of a contemporary history of civilizations . . . But the practice of world history in a global age does reconfigure the field in which these paradigms are deployed.'[13]

An overview

This book is a contribution to the process of understanding world history. Benefiting from an analysis developed in the study of civilizations and world systems, it offers an overview of global history in terms of the three groups of problems that have the greatest impact on historical change. These are the economic problems of subsistence and surplus, the political problems of stability and security, and finally the religious or ideological problems to do with our understanding of self, society and salvation. It is the argument of this book that this core group of problems provides not just a perspective on world history, but an insight into some important parallels between civilizations.

In comparing civilizations it has become clear that there have been parallels in terms both of stages of growth and the key problems that have been faced at each stage. These parallels suggest a framework for the study of civilizations that consists of three phases (formation, expansion, limitation) and the interplay of three factors (economics, politics, belief). The underlying theme is that, while all the factors are important in all the phases, their *relative* importance changes from one phase to the next. Thus, in the formative period the economic factors of subsistence and surplus are paramount; in the period of enlargement the political factors of power and control are paramount; and in the period of limitation the ideological factors of belief and commitment are paramount. Given this changing pattern of emphasis, the other factors are generally seen to provide more of a supportive role.

This relationship between phases and factors provides a framework for studying civilizations separately, for tracing similarities between them, and for comparing which of the factors of economics, politics and belief had the most significance at each stage. Throughout the experience of the civilizations, economic, political and ideological factors have of course always been present, but what is significant is that first one and then another became more important in relation to the main problems of the time. When a movement of peoples leads to settlement and surplus there are some common consequences. With better living the population increases, with more consumption there is need for more material resources; to secure them and defend them the frame is enlarged. In time the enlargement of the frame creates new problems: the relationship of the expanding periphery to the centre, and of expanding societies with each other and with more mobile or nomadic groups. New political structures are attempted and some succeed, providing for a time a common rule over diverse peoples. When the imperial structures become overextended there is political breakdown; cohesion is achieved less by means of politics and increasingly by means of ideology or religion. This common experience, which is found in the classical civilizations as much as in early modern and contemporary civilizations, may be represented in a simple grid (see overleaf).

A further theme of this study is that technology has a key relationship to all the factors, although it is first and most obviously seen in relation to economics and the tools and techniques necessary to sustain settlements and cities. The term is used throughout in its broadest sense to include any means, processes or skills of a technical nature to achieve particular ends. As such it includes the making of pots as well as the technical aspects of controlling behaviour or spreading knowledge.

The themes and the framework just outlined allow for the key developments in the history of a civilization to be outlined in the space of a paragraph. In the case of American

Phases	Factors	Key problems
Formation	<u>Economic</u> Political Ideological	Problems of subsistence, surplus and specialization, including the tools and techniques needed for production, distribution and exchange within and between settled regions
Expansion	<u>Political</u> Economic Ideological	Problems of authority and security and the relationship between the core and periphery areas as well as frontier issues which require a military and most typically imperial solution
Limitation	<u>Ideological</u> Economic Political	Problems of identity and cohesion as political and military structures begin to break up, leading to attempts at spiritual/ideological allegiance within and beyond imperial boundaries

civilization, for example, the first colonists faced an immediate need for adequate and continuing subsistence. With the creation of a surplus above that level, more permanent settlements became possible. This required not just a productive economy but also a durable political structure and an ideological commitment. Precisely because these became part of the American experience, the enterprise succeeded. But in its very success lay further problems: the political problems of relations between the centre and the parts, and between the new nation and other nations. These problems dominated the history of America from the Declaration of Independence to the outcome of the Civil War. They were resolved by political means, but with the help of industrial technology and an ideology which overruled divisive tendencies. In the twentieth century, however, separatist tendencies again engaged the American people as they tested the limits of their growth in ideological causes.

In common with all the earlier civilizations, America's has encountered a recurrent tension between movement and settlement, becoming in the process a frontier society dotted with townships. At all times in all the regions there has been both the ongoing search for subsistence in varying habitats and the desire to make permanent the particular relationships between peoples and their homesteads. The settlers in the first civilizations, and centuries later in the early modern civilizations, no matter how committed they were to their permanent centres, were nevertheless impelled to go beyond them: at first prospecting for raw materials, then in a need for security behind extending frontiers, and finally in the missionary motivation of the would-be universal churches. This recurrent pattern has been an integral part of global history: through the sequences of the regional civilizations, and in the interactions between them and with peoples still following a nomadic path. In all the phases and in all the factors there have been encounters with other societies. There have been patterns of exchange and exploitation, patterns of conquest and military rule, and patterns of missionary conviction and endeavour. Exchange, conquest and belief have been the recurrent modes through which human societies have influenced each other and their common global habitat.

It is within the sequences of the civilizations, and in the manifestations of the factors which govern their corporate existence, that the tension between movement and settlement has repeatedly thrown up global tendencies. These have all in essence been attempts to resolve the tension on an ever-widening scale, achieving patterns of coexistence between the societies while each sought to preserve the harmony and drive of its own heritage and aspiration. When these attempts lost momentum and foundered there were periods of lost direction and fading vision until the sequences could be re-enacted and the balance of the factors restored.

The narrative

The structure of the book reflects the argument. In part I, the focus is on the resources, on the economic needs which impelled our distant ancestors on their global odyssey and, many millennia later, laid the groundwork for permanent centres. I show how rulers and myth-makers provided support for the primary concern of an economic surplus. In part II, the political structures become all-important in resolving the problems of hostile encounters, and key improvements in the networks of communication (highways, alphabets, coinages) provided the means to harness the global impulses of the empires. In their success however lay the seeds of their decline, and they paid the price of overextension. It was then, as related in part III, that the spiritual imperative took over, in a renewed search for common purposes which overran the political frontiers.

In part IV, the story is resumed in the further massive movement of peoples which occurred between the end of the ancient world and the beginnings of the modern world. Between the two lay several centuries of economic arrest or decline and the loss of stable political structures. In the process continuity suffered, as in the break between classical Mediterranean civilization and a new civilization to the north in western Europe. In a similar way there was a break between classical civilization based on the north China plain and a new civilization based on the river system and coastal area in the south. These two new civilizations, which I have called early modern, began around the same time as civilizations based on the fertilization of the eastern Slavlands by the Vikings and the Arabic fertilization of the Middle East. In these four regions economic advance, supported by alliances between political and religious leaderships, led to new civilized centres which drew on the experience of the past, but more significantly on their own technological innovation. In part V, the global impulse is resumed in the empires of the

Chinese, the Russians, the Muslims, and the western Europeans. Advances in the tools of empire, particularly in shipbuilding and weaponry, prepared the way for industrial revolution; and revolutionary ideas, of nationalism and of progress, moved out disturbingly along the seaways. Finally, in part VI, we look at the global systems of the modern era, the evolution of a world economy, the hostile encounters of the last two centuries, and the communication networks we are still busily creating.

The global history of the last millennium is based on a comparison of the early modern civilizations of China, Russia, Islam and western Europe, all of which in the twentieth century reached phases of limitation. Their empires failed to command the commitment of their diverse peoples, and despite the improvements in communications, intensive propaganda and military power, they all experienced crises of growth. This was a global phenomenon in which two more modern civilizations have increasingly played a part as America and Japan have moved towards expanding hegemonies. Entering into a world economic system already taking shape, they have become leading promoters of multinational enterprise and global communication. In this context, a brief overview of global history must take into account the interrelated roles of the six modern civilizations in a global model rather than a Eurocentric one.

While using for convenience the familiar terms we know as civilizations and empires, I have tried to avoid giving them a reality they do not possess. It was groups of people around the globe who found ways of resolving problems that enabled some core areas to achieve permanence as the basis for high achievement in the arts of living. From the core areas, knowledge of the achievement spread widely and there was contact between groups. There were hostile encounters and means found to deal with them. But the solving of problems, the achievement of better living, the spread of knowledge, and the hostile encounters, were all the work of people, of people working together in groups for common ends. If from time to time we label all this in terms of civilizations and empires and world systems, it does not mean that these were in some sense entities, capable of solving problems, conferring better living, having encounters. It was human beings who did these things, following impulses to become civilized, to become globalized. They, and their impulses, are the subject of the story told in these pages.

This is not a book in which to look things up, but a book that offers a perspective on global history, or rather the several perspectives of economics, politics and ideology in global history. The main interest has been in the making of broad comparisons, not with any intention of arguing for a kind of historical determinism, but certainly with the intention of offering some reasoned generalizations. If globalization is an idea whose time has come, it is because the trends of the past have come together. But if the idea is ever to become a reality in a truly global society, all the factors would have to be satisfied. As well as an economic foundation there would have to be a workable political structure and a recognition of common purpose.

NOTES

1 P. Mellars and C. Stringer, eds, *The Human Revolution*, Edinburgh University Press, 1989, p. 26.
2 D. Held, A. McGrew, D. Goldblatt and J. Perraton, *Global Transformations*, Polity, 1999, p. 1.
3 A. J. Toynbee, *A Study of History*, 12 vols, Oxford University Press, 1934–1961.
4 W. H. McNeill, *The Rise of the West*, Chicago University Press, 1963.
5 W. H. McNeill, 'The changing shape of world history', in *World History*, ed. P. Pomper, R. H. Elphick and R. T. Vann, Blackwell, 1998, pp. 28, 29.
6 I. Wallerstein, *The Modern World-System*, vol. 1, Academic Press, 1974, p. 349.
7 Ibid., p. 15.
8 B. Mazlish and B. Buultjens, eds, *Conceptualizing Global History*, Westview, 1993.
9 Held et al., *Global Transformations*, p. 13.

10 A. G. Frank and B. K. Gills, eds, *The World System*, Routledge, 1993.
11 Peter Worsley, *The Three Worlds*, Weidenfeld and Nicolson, 1984.
12 Held et al., *Global Transformations*, p. 12.
13 M. Geyer and C. Bright, 'World history in a global age', *American Historical Review* 100 (Oct. 1995).

THE CLASSICAL ERA

PART I
The Primary Concern

Between 100 millennia and 10 millennia ago our ancestors penetrated all the continents of the earth. The search was for suitable habitats yielding an adequate subsistence. About two-thirds of the way through that period, radical changes occurred in parts of Europe in the making and use of stone tools. They were accompanied by changes in social organization and mental concepts, as illustrated for example in cave paintings. By the end of the period, in parts of the Middle East the hunting economy had passed into a farming economy and the preconditions had been met for creating the permanent civilized centres of the classical era. These appeared over a period from five millennia ago in several sites across the Old World and in Mesoamerica and Peru. The need for subsistence was still the primary concern, and provision for it was supported by the way community life was organized and by the beliefs that grew around it.

1
Global Odyssey

Searching for Subsistence

The available evidence of fossils, stone age tools and, more recently, molecular genetics suggests that an archaic African population of some 200,000 years ago provided the source from which anatomically modern human beings (our ancestors) developed by 100,000 years ago. Dispersal would seem to be the mechanism for their appearance in the rest of the world. Separate evolution in different regions has been considered, but is thought to be implausible and difficult to reconcile with the molecular data. A new species entering a new habitat would have had an advantage over locally conditioned stock by reason of its more generalized exploitation of the environment. It is possible that some limited interbreeding provided for an element of regional continuity. But the African evidence taken as a whole does indicate the presence there of essentially modern human beings extending back to 100,000 years before the present, and this is the most useful and reliable place to begin an account of the human odyssey.

Subsistence came mainly at that time from preying on other animals and, in a fluctuating savannah zone of interacting plant and animal populations, a successful niche was found dependent on a large and varied range of mammals. A limited acquisition of hunting techniques would have served to establish the human stock. In time, some improvement of the basic tool-kit and the use of fire probably damaged the vegetation and increased the pressure on the

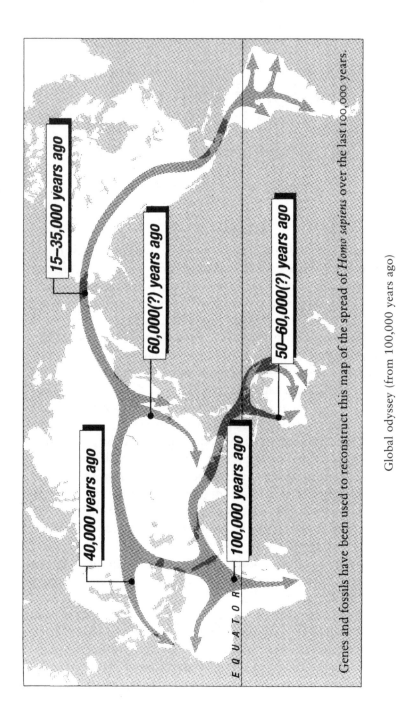

15–35,000 years ago

60,000(?) years ago

50–60,000(?) years ago

40,000 years ago

100,000 years ago

E Q U A T O R

Global odyssey (from 100,000 years ago)

Genes and fossils have been used to reconstruct this map of the spread of *Homo sapiens* over the last 100,000 years.

Source: C. Stringer and R. McKie, *African Exodus*, Pimlico, 1996, p. 169, based on Akio Morishima, *Book of Life*.

animal populations (even perhaps in some instances to the point of extinction), while the human populations grew in size and extended their territorial range. From its origin in forager society the family became the universal phenomenon in human societies. It was the smallest and most natural viable economic unit. It was also the vehicle through which society grew as the characteristic form of human organization and extension. It seems likely that small forager bands based on the extended family would have found advantage in wider associations, looser perhaps at first, for exchange and social activities. In the success of this strategy lay the potential for population growth and the consequent demand for more territory.

In intervals when the climate became less favourable – to humans and to other species – the search for subsistence turned into migration, at first in Africa and subsequently beyond. In a preference for habitats with similar climates, fauna and flora, parts of the Middle East and India were occupied, and eventually south-east Asia when a return to cold conditions reduced the area of tropical rainforests. Lower sea levels gave easier access to Australia and pursuit of animal herds took some hunters across the Bering straits into America. The likely timescale for the global odyssey is that an exodus from Africa began soon after 100,000 years ago, probably using the hospitable Nile valley as a corridor into Asia, reaching New Guinea and Australia about 50,000 years ago, and a little later dispersing westward from Asia and reaching Europe. Between 35,000 and 15,000 years ago Asian tribes crossed into Alaska and began the 9,000 mile trek that led their descendants through rainforests, across deserts and over mountains to the extreme south of the American continent.

Such wide expansion over formidable physical barriers and over so many thousands of years is thought to have been motivated primarily by population growth as succeeding generations sought more foraging territory for their support. By no means could this always have been a smooth and peaceful process. Struggles with other populations, of other species and of the same or other hominid groups, would have entailed hardship and violence and failures and disasters of which no record remains. Success depended often and critically on deployment of skills and degrees of commitment, in the beginnings of group organization and beliefs that were later to characterize the formation of permanently settled societies. Foraging groups in various parts of the world have been shown to exhibit technical innovation, occupational specialization, social inequality and conceptual maturity in the emergence of an increased cultural complexity.

Between 30,000 and 40,000 years ago, major changes occurred in both the anatomy of human populations and the technology of associated assemblages over large areas of Europe and the immediately adjacent areas of north-east Africa and south-west Asia. There were at least three significant aspects of change: rapid shifts in the structure of tools from flake to blade production, standardization of the deliberately imposed form in shaping tools, and a greater complexity of patterning in relation to social factors and levels of perception. At about the same time, cave paintings, rock engravings and decorated objects began to appear in Europe; and among the most vivid representations were those of the large game animals with which the hunting communities had the most intimate relationship. Symbolism, magic and mythic significance have been seen in the subject-matter and its treatment.

Evidence of these profound changes is clearest in Europe, where our ancestors at that time faced some appalling conditions towards the end of the last ice age. It is the area where most research has been done, but there is enough from elsewhere to suggest that other parts of the Old World were experiencing cultural upheaval. Australia had been colonized by people from south-east Asia who were making paintings and engravings and using mature burial features. Both the Australian desert and the Siberian arctic tundra were challenging environments demanding social and conceptual changes if human life was to survive. It was these changes rather than the new technologies alone which allowed the occupation of areas which were low in resource density, diversity and – especially in Siberia – predictability. Contact and movement between hunting groups were essential to pass information quickly and take prompt decisions. Kinship and other alliances increased language competence in the discussion of available options. Without such responses to extreme circumstances, the migration from Siberia to America would be difficult to conceive.

In the search for security, more sedentary lifestyles were sometimes adopted, causing different habitats to be favoured. The positive characteristics of a prime hunting domain were an equable climate, adequate water and numerous fauna and flora. Good settlement conditions also included fertile soils and the presence of edible wild plants and herbivores, which were likely to be found near rivers and the sea. With the use of rafts and canoes, entire seaboards were open to colonization, and hilly country which generated springs or streams was also in demand. With the extension of habitats went innovations in diet and food-gathering techniques. Flesh-eating hunters, while accepting that vegetation was primarily food for game, also consumed parts of plants such as nuts, fruits and seeds. In areas where yams and gourds and the like were plentiful, dependence on plants eventually overtook animal foods.

An increasing reliance by foragers on wild cereals encouraged a more sedentary habit which led to the exploitation of other local resources including small animals. The advent of semi-permanent sites marked an increasing sedentism and eventually some permanent villages and population increase. In localities where human groups congregated for periods of time, the surroundings were cleared and opened up. More attention was given to plant growth and renewal, leading to selection and weeding and cultivation; and where human densities were high and sites were limited there were motives for the more sustained labour of digging, processing and protection. Different tools were required, and more versatile tool use acted as a stimulus to mental and linguistic activity, to changing patterns of social behaviour, and to attitudes towards territory. Sources of water needed to be guarded, and less nomadic habits encouraged more niches to be occupied. The tendency towards demographic expansion and the wider diffusion of tools and techniques raised issues relating to neighbouring groups.

By ten millennia ago human beings as hunters were in all the continents and hunting was still their dominant role. The surface of the earth, while adapted to the needs of a vast game park, was however marked by sedentary adaptations. By five millennia ago, the domestication of plants and animals was widespread and cultivators were established in virtually all parts of the Old World. A particular combination of climatic, environmental and biological conditions had appeared first near the meeting place of Asia, Africa and Europe. Similar sequences of development in widely separated areas – including Mesoamerica and Peru – make it likely that the beginnings of agriculture occurred independently. With it came the slow accumulation and transmission of a culture of interacting techniques, institutions and beliefs. In place of the once popular notion of an agricultural revolution, opinion now inclines to a more evolutionary process of mixed economies and experiments, in which domesticates were initially a supplement to existing foodstuffs in areas with an abundance of resources.

The primacy of one region, from the Levant to the Zagros mountains, is however accepted. Here there was a natural and well-established distribution of wild strains of barley and wheat and suitable grazing for sheep and goats. In an overlap of the ranges of these plants and animals, cattle were first domesticated. It was an area sufficient in density and extent to promote a sedentary habit. With increasing site adaptation, the needs of irrigation were met by channelling, and eventually canal construction. In the Nile valley and the Mediterranean, similar transitions occurred, with some limited influence between the areas. Soon afterwards, the experiment was repeated on the great plains of the Indus and on the bends of the Yellow River in China where millet and later rice were cultivated. In Mesoamerica and Peru, maize was the most suitable plant for cultivation. Cereals became the basis everywhere of a self-amplifying system, first harvested in their natural state and cultivated when populations expanded beyond what this could sustain. Stable on an annual basis, they were a rich source of protein and calories which could be easily and reliably stored. Pottery vessels appeared suddenly by 8,000 years ago in wide areas of the Old World, from North Africa through the Middle East to Japan.

The association of villages with cultivation was also a global phenomenon. From the camp sites with which hunter-gatherers were familiar, there was a transition around 7,000 years ago to semi-permanent base camps. With the coming of agriculture, permanent occupation was needed all year, with habitations suited to all seasons grouped around common facilities. While temporary quarters continued at particular task locations, the village pattern crystallized as the basic unit of occupation in all regions of the world. With the extension of cultivation, more villages could be budded off, creating a network of communities along lines of water supply and fertility. Successful settlement attracted more people from less successful areas, as well as from nomad groups of food gatherers and pastoralists.

By 5,000 years ago the first city societies were beginning to flourish in Mesopotamia, and the cooperation of farming communities along the Nile had led to a single kingdom along its length. In the Indus region, peasant groups from the foothills were settling along the river, while in the grassy uplands mobile pastoralists grazed their herds and traded with itinerant hunter-gatherers. In China, below the southern bend of the Yellow River, villages were raising pigs and harvesting grain, while inner Asia was the domain of pastoral nomads whose influence reached across wide areas of steppe and led to occasional warlike migrations. Communities in central and western Mediterranean Europe were still partly reliant on wild resources but were beginning to practise farming, while trade in the Aegean was raising living standards and encouraging a civilizing tendency on the island of Crete.

In north Africa a 'wet phase' encouraged a mixing of peoples and the raising of herds of horned cattle, and when the region dried out the farmers moved south into west Africa. In the New World the first humans had found extensive herds of large grazing animals and were developing their own weapons and tools for dealing with them. In north America soon after 5,000 years ago some groups were cultivating plants such as sunflowers and squashes. The Australian coastline was established by that time and wandering aboriginals were gathering what food they could find, clearing areas of bush to encourage new growth, and hunting species of big game until they became extinct. They had invented the boomerang, together with some small fine stone tools.

The balance between movement and settlement of communities was still very fluid and the settlements in most regions outside the civilized centres were of a temporary nature. Regional and local migration brought different peoples into contact, leading to some mixing, particularly in the favoured areas of settlement.

A survey in the central Euphrates flood plain has disclosed that the population increased tenfold in about two centuries, with a wholesale movement into the area. In early historical times, there were two separate sources of ethnic and linguistic material in Mesopotamia, Sumerian and Semitic, the mixture providing a potential for future cultural advance. Among the earliest pottery styles is evidence of influences from Syria and Iran. In the Ubaid phase, which was crucial in the build-up to civilization, invaders came in several waves.

The arrival of new people in the Nile valley (from Mesopotamia, Syria or Iran) significantly stimulated the pace of development there. The earliest farming settlements above the plains of the Indus may have been associated with the arrival of more advanced communities, and wheat and barley were introduced into northern China from west and central Asia. In America, the steady drift of populations from north to south brought some of them to regions where big game were scarce and alternative means of subsistence were needed. An area of early settlement in Mesoamerica featured winding rivers and fertile soil, from which village farming spread on to higher ground and into the lowlands towards the Gulf of Mexico.

The coming of civilization is associated with a range of activities such as pottery, textiles, building, metallurgy and a maturing tool-kit in complex evolving societies across Eurasia. Writing was often among these, taking various forms in different areas but nearly always associated with the keeping of accounts, and tending to spread rapidly in the service of trade. Writing systems which recorded the spoken language were also used by the Maya people in what may have been a development across Mesoamerica. Major developments in architecture in virtually all the civilizing centres were among the more obvious signs of an economic surplus and a division of labour.

The surplus itself was crucially associated with maturing skills in the management of water supplies. Irrigation had first been practised systematically on a small scale in the upland villages and small plains, where runnels to vegetable plots became widened into ditches. With growing confidence, it was extended downstream into the swampy and erratic delta of the Tigris–Euphrates system, and something similar may be presumed to have occurred soon after in north-west India and northern China. In Mesoamerica and the Andean region, artificial canals appeared early in the sequences, and bolder undertakings tapped the fertility of lakeside areas, as well as linking up river valleys. Over generations, skills in water control increased to the point where nutrient-rich soils were yielding surpluses large enough to extend the centres of civilization.

2

Civilized Centres

Settlements Become Permanent

The civilized centres which grew out of the villages and towns drew on the surpluses to provide more permanent and complex societies. The simplest of agricultural peoples needed a surplus, at least to provide the seed corn, but in the civilized centres the sheer size of the surplus appears to have been significant, taken in conjunction with the uses to which it was put. People needed confidence to undertake urban planning, to keep records, to embark on monumental enterprises. They needed to believe that their society had a future, not just anywhere but in this particular place; and in particular places the cores of regional societies were created, in the Middle East, in the eastern Mediterranean, in India, China, Mexico and Peru. Widely different in the processes of their growth and in their basic characteristics, all the regional civilizations depended on viable economies, effective political arrangements and common beliefs. The economic systems, and the technology which drove them, were initially of major importance. The civilizations might more appropriately be called ecological zones, in which there was contact between human groups and considerable movement in the boundaries of the areas occupied.

Permanent settlement required more than subsistence. Raw materials were needed for tools and buildings and household equipment, and these had usually to be brought from further afield. Restricted distribution meant that transport and trading were required over considerable distances. The settlers in the Nile sent expeditions south to quarry stone and north to the Sinai peninsula to mine copper. City builders in the Tigris–Euphrates basin exploited the forested sides of the mountains and scoured the lands beyond for mineral deposits. In central America, centuries later, the Olmec people sent groups into the highlands for raw materials and into distant regions for jade, and from the city of Teotihuacan traders went into most of central Mexico and further south for the resources of its obsidian industry. In virtually all the civilized centres, a balance had to be struck between settlement and mobility.

By 3000 BC, the technologies favourable to the beginning of civilization had been assembled in suitable sites. Along the final course of the Euphrates, city societies began to flourish, separated from each other by desert and marsh, each concerned to protect its cherished resource of fertilized land and provide some protection for the rural population. This was the homeland of Sumerian civilization, with perhaps some partly independent and parallel developments to the east in Elam. In the basin of the two rivers, there was an occasional excess of flooding and a tendency for the alluvial soils to deteriorate through increased salinity; but the greatly enlarged surplus and the emergence of military leadership provided long enough intervals of seeming permanence for all the features of civilized centres to appear. Other centres have been found, dated to the end of the millennium, which were obviously based, not on soil and water as such, but on trade routes between the major areas of settlement.

Native copper was smelted in the mountain chain from which the Tigris–Euphrates system of rivers emanated and where the richest mineral deposits were found. There were no raw material supplies in the delta, the growth of population there continued to stimulate demand and, after a thousand years, the older sources were running thin. A crisis of supply would have affected both the urban consumers and the itinerant miners, smelters and smiths who met their needs. It seems likely that there would have been a further outward movement in search particularly of copper and tin deposits. There was a long period of encroachment on the northern lands of Sumer by Semitic peoples known as Akkadians in attempts to secure by trade or conquest the essential raw materials.

Meanwhile, civilization had also taken root in the Nile valley, but in entirely different circumstances. Compared to the open and exposed nature of the Tigris–Euphrates basin, the Egyptian habitat was enclosed by desert and mountains which provided from the start a sense of permanence. There were some settled communities during the fourth millennium, based on mixed farming and enjoying some trading contacts. It is thought that newcomers may have fused with the local population, providing a stimulus for technological advance which led to writing, monumental architecture and distinctive art forms.

Cooperation between the riverside communities was crucial. The Nile valley at that time was probably marshy and overgrown, requiring a system of drains and canals to allow intensive cultivation to take place. The potential was such that, once this was achieved, substantial economic surpluses would have been available. By the beginning of the dynastic period in 3100 BC it is likely that the necessary conditions existed for planning and disciplined preparation over a considerable length of the river. It was during the Old Kingdom from 2686 to 2181 BC that the great pyramids were constructed, a feat that would not have been possible without surplus resources.

There can be little doubt that such exercises presented an immense strain on the economy. So great in fact was the burden that it eventually proved counterproductive and contributed to the breakdown of society. This was followed by the first intermediate period, a shattering discontinuity for a people to whom a sense of permanence and security had come more easily than elsewhere and had seemed by the predictable beneficence of the river to be so fully justified. When civilized life returned to Egypt it was with a passionate aversion to change.

Meanwhile, there had been a quickening of activity around the Aegean Sea, in mainland Greece, in the Cyclades and in Crete. Greece at that time provided a contrast in economic terms between the rich grain areas in Thessaly and the coastal areas in the south, where vine and olive cultivation flourished. In the third millennium BC, the centre of population and prosperity swung to the south, where fish and legumes were joining the staples of the Mediterranean diet and a metal industry was stimulating trade and communications. The Cyclades and Crete were closely linked in the development of artefacts, and Crete, with a particularly favourable agricultural environment, was leading the way in maritime trade in the Mediterranean.

Whether by settlement or by local initiative, Crete had a variety of crops and farm animals and its own pottery tradition. In the third millennium BC, stimulated perhaps by contact with the other civilizations, there was a far greater pace of change. The base of the economic surplus was the 'Mediterranean triad' of grain, olives and vines. Profiting from the rich markets of the Levant and Egypt, the Minoans (as they were known, from the legendary leader Minos) created a civilization that was all their own. At several sites and over at least six centuries, and in that time often rebuilt, the Minoan palaces were constructed on generous lines, with lavish rooms and pillared corridors richly adorned; and there were elegant villas and mansions all over the countryside. This was a remarkably peaceful and relaxed society, with centralized control over its agriculture, trade and industry. In 1700 BC, however, it was shattered by an earthquake. It was rebuilt, but was overwhelmed again around 1500 BC by a cataclysm from which it never fully recovered. About 1375 BC, the surviving city of Knossos fell, presumably to enemy attack, and Crete became subject to the mainland power of Mycenae, which had been growing in strength for several centuries. Here, as in Mesopotamia and Egypt, though for different reasons, the precariousness of civilization had been underlined.

The Indus valley in north-west India shared with the Nile and the Euphrates ample supplies of flood-borne silt, which encouraged peasant groups to move from the foothills and acquire the arts of water management. In villages just above the flood-line, they were able, during the third millennium BC, to accumulate sufficient surpluses of wheat and barley to embark on what became the early Harappan culture. Based on the two cities of upstream Harappa and downstream Mohenjodaro, the Indus civilization in its mature phase extended over half a million square miles of Sind and Punjab, and as such lasted into the next millennium. By 2000 BC, cotton was being spun and woven into cloth, a number of other specialized crafts had been established, and there were trade links with Afghanistan, Iran and Mesopotamia.

The major cities were constructed on a grid plan, with efficient main drainage, dominated by a citadel. The largest and most remarkable building in Harappa was the 'great granary', and the most striking in Mohenjodaro was the 'great bath'. The extent of the built-up areas and the technical competence required, the evidence of long-term planning and the keeping of commercial records amply confirm that the economic surplus was sufficient to leave a margin for communal investment after providing for the basic material needs of a large and growing population. The Indus society was, however, overtaken by catastrophe in the second millennium BC as a result of flooding or invasion, bequeathing possible connections to the civilization which later arose in the Ganges region.

A little later than the early Harappan culture, there were farming settlements in north China with some of the ingredients for civilization. It is thought that different ethnic groups contributed to the outcome. The earliest agriculture was practised in the central valley of the Hwang-ho river system, where the yellow loess soil, blown out of central Asia some millions of years before, provided an easily worked source of fertility. About 2500 BC, a rapidly growing population appeared in this area and was enabled by surplus food production to expand eastward along the course of the river.

This was too far north apparently for rice culture, which may by then have appeared in south China but did not at that time provide for the beginnings of civilization. Between wooded highlands and lowland swamps, millet could be grown amid an abundance of plant and animal life. The Chou people, who had interacted with nomads, finally became dominant, with a merging of skills and ruling elites.

A thousand years later than in China, the beginnings of civilized centres had appeared in Mesoamerica and Peru alongside farming villages. From an independent site in the Gulf Coast heartland, the influence of the Olmec people spread widely. Deriving an economic surplus from an area of rich alluvial soil and abundant rainfall, it became a source of civilization on which the Maya civilization was ultimately dependent. The mainstays of life were maize farming and fishing. From their centre at San Lorenzo, characterized by massive stone monuments, the Olmec people sent groups into the highlands in what appears to have been a route to obtain raw materials and luxury items for their landowning elite. They had settlements in distant regions, especially where jade was found, with evidence of military and possibly missionary activity.

The Chavin culture, which covered most of the north and centre of Peru, had some resemblances to Egyptian culture in the ceremonial centres which acted as focuses for scattered sites. The maize crop was apparently introduced by highland intruders and there is evidence of early canals and other agrarian works. The Chavin art style, exemplified in its pottery and temple artefacts, spread rapidly, ending the regional isolation of the initial period as immigrant people imposed their religion and political control on earlier inhabitants. Temple construction was directed by a small number of skilled craftsmen, directing pilgrims to work tasks as they assembled for the observance of festivals, possibly in connection with an oracle.

Whatever contacts there may have been between the civilized centres, their establishment with basically similar features, from the eastern Mediterranean through the Middle

East to India and China and (after a time lag) through central
America into the Andean region of Peru, is compelling evidence of a widespread and persistent desire, following the
global odyssey, to settle in favoured areas and make settlement permanent. Mobility was a part of that process, and
it remained a feature of the settlements in the context
both of their need for raw materials and to sustain the
larger populations which higher productivity encouraged.
The two impulses were to ride together down the long ages
that lay ahead, the characteristics of a species that had
explored the global habitat and wished to make its occupation permanent.

Common problems of continuing subsistence and economic surplus, of finding and exploiting resources of raw
materials, of developing techniques of transportation and
trade, were resolved in similar ways in societies which in
other ways exhibited remarkably dissimilar features and
tendencies. Furthermore, in all of them, solving the economic problem called also for supporting solutions to political problems. One was concerned with the maintenance of
internal order and commitment to common purposes. The
other was concerned with encounters with groups outside the
civilized centres. In the next two chapters, it will be shown
that in these respects also there were remarkable correspondences across the whole global phenomenon.

3

Rulers and Myths

Preconditions of Stability

For a long time before villages grew into towns and towns into cities, some authority would have been required to convert peasant leisure into an economic surplus, to make people work harder than they wanted in order to provide for future needs and communal commitments. With the steady movement towards more complicated tasks, there came more division of labour and a strengthening of some form of central control. This was likely to have been the first major political consequence of the coming of civilized centres. The role of the city was very different from one core area to another: in Mesopotamia the result of sprawling populations growing by steady accretions, in India more regular in concept and plan, in Egypt exclusively for religious and administrative purposes, in Crete palace societies with a more secular character. What they had in common was a social complexity, arising from the interdependence of specialized groups, the provision of common services and the acceptance of an impersonal authority, which could be economic, military or religious, or any combination of these. Imposed as it were on the basic ecological zone, there was increasingly a political context and the beginnings of a cultural community.

The need to regularize trade between urban centres and the communities around and beyond their peripheries led to a further political consequence. Elements of civilized culture were tending to be diffused outwards to groups which were both dependent on the cities and provided for some of their needs, exchanging for example the products of pastoralism or quarrying for manufactures. Sooner or later the question of authority over such groups would arise in the context of stability and security. In the Mesopotamian zone the ever expanding search for supplies of materials, at first for stone and timber and later for copper and tin, and the development of reciprocal trade would have called for commercial and planning agencies effective over wide areas and long periods of time. Defence of the towns and the trading networks was also needed against the always restless nomads: and defence would sometimes turn into attack when there was an opportunity to bring under control new areas to be farmed or mined. There had to be an authority which could recruit, maintain, train and equip a military force.

In all these comings and goings involving the exercise of authority, the rulers of the early civilizations were prone to invoke the approval of the gods. Perhaps in our sense of the word they were not gods at all, but rather the symbolic expression of the custom and consent of the political community. The gods were an added dimension, the pride and hope of the people spirited forth and given a form larger than life, manifesting themselves through rulers who exercised power by proxy. There was in effect a hierarchy of authority, linking men and gods in a continuous chain. At first, no doubt, power was allowed only to particular leaders, for specific tasks and for limited periods; but powers granted in an emergency would sometimes linger on. Rulers over wider areas could have become rather remote beings, exercising their authority perhaps through functional or territorial representatives, while they themselves acquired charisma and made bids for immortality.

The evolution of the new political forms and the emergence of the new spiritual concepts were indivisible processes, aspects almost of the same process. When the people of that time made statements about divinity, about the numinous, about their dependence upon and subservience to beings beyond their reach and comprehension, they were extrapolating from their own political experience. Just as their course of technological innovation had led them step by step into a series of essays in government, so did the latter in turn lead them into fresh conceptual adventures. Cumulatively, their civilizations had been prodigious acts of creation, and this was embodied figuratively in local creation stories which displayed some marked common features from one society to another, such as the substitution of order for chaos, the control of the waters and the safeguarding of the annual fertility. The myths postulated primeval beings of great power and originality, treating as godlike the achievements of people over many generations; they established beliefs thought to be necessary to perpetuate the well-being which the new technology had made possible. Earthly authority was derived from the gods, and within and alongside the religious myths testaments emerged in each society which authorized political power and required political obedience.

Sargon of Agade was the first great conqueror known to history, the founder of an empire lasting for a century and a half (2334–2154 BC). The *Chronicles Concerning Sargon* recorded: 'Unto Sargon, king of the land, the god Enlil gave, no one opposing, from the upper sea to the lower sea . . . Sargon, king of the lands of the earth.' The greatest military leader of ancient Egypt was Thutmose III (1490–1436 BC). *The Hymn of Victory* recorded the Utterance of Amon-Re, the god of Thebes: 'I have given to thee might and victory against all countries. I have set thy fame, even the fear of thee, in all lands. The chiefs of all countries are gathered in thy grasp.' King Wen was the legendary founder of the Chou dynasty in China (1171–1122 BC). *The Book of Odes* recorded: 'The Mandate of Heaven, how beautiful and unceasing! O, how glorious was the purity of King Wen's virtue! With blessings he overwhelms us. We will receive his blessings.'

The patterns of belief of the early civilizations contained much that was inherited from earlier stages of human experience, in particular the concern for fertility and an interest in life after death. What was new about the conceptual concerns were firstly the process of creation itself, and secondly the problem of authority to which it gave rise. Thousands of years had gone into this increasingly elaborate form of human society, and for thousands of years afterwards the folk memory of the achievement persisted in the religious traditions of many different peoples. The creation myths featured prominently in the earliest literature of Mesopotamia, Egypt and India, and some have been carried over into still living traditions. So old are some of these writings that their origins cannot be dated and an older oral tradition is implied; yet they can still catch the imagination and affect the outlook of the twentieth century.

The Sumerian scripture speaks in its opening lines of a time when the firm ground had not been established and the fresh and salt waters had not been separated. In Egypt, the idea of a primeval ocean was present from the earliest times: out of the water arose the primeval earth hill which bore the first living being. In the Genesis version, the earth was at first without form and void, until the spirit moved upon the face of the waters and they were gathered together and the dry land was allowed to appear. In the Vedic version, there was at first 'undiscriminated chaos' and mighty waters containing the 'universal germ', until the earth's begetter brought forth 'the great and lucid waters', after which desire arose and with it the primal need. The Chinese account also has a primeval period of chaos when the 'waters inundated without being stopped', followed by a period of universal harmony when the wild waters were checked.

The waters having been brought under control, the land was then made fruitful. In the Sumerian pantheon, it was Enlil, the father of the gods, who brought forth the seed from the land in the form of trees and grain. The god of Genesis said, 'let the earth bring forth grass, the herb yielding seed, and the fruit trees yielding fruit', and made man to have dominion over all living things. In Egypt, the pharaohs were believed to control the annual rise and fall of the river, and the first known rituals of Egyptian kingship were concerned with irrigation and land reclamation. The Chinese myth has a divine being named Yu, descending from on high and creating a habitable world for mankind. Thus the gods who came to personify the new technology of water control and agriculture represented both the process itself and the generations of humans who had been inspired to carry it into effect.

The second major concern was the allocation of authority and its reconciliation with religious belief. A common characteristic of the civilized centres was a recognition of the separate realms of political and spiritual authority. At the same time there were attempts, varying according to circumstances, to align them behind the primary concerns of economic viability. Sometimes there was outright identification, as in the divine kingship of the Egyptians or the plurality of functions focused on the Chinese rulers. Sometimes it was an elite class from which leadership cadres were recruited, as in the Olmec state in central America or Chavin society in Peru. In all the centres there appeared to be a search for general principles which linked particular circumstances and local formulae to overriding cosmic phenomena. For the Sumerians, human society was seen to be modelled with exact correspondences on divine society; for the Chinese a supreme deity overlooked the earthly authority and removed it if it failed; in Mesoamerica the moral order remained intact when political control lapsed or frontiers shifted.

From the earliest times, the local shrine in Sumerian cities was important as a focus of community loyalty. Not unnaturally, it often became the centre for the collection and distribution of the economic surplus, of foodstuffs and the products of craft work and trade; and by the time writing appeared as a means of recording these transactions the shrine had developed into the temple. This did not necessarily mean an increase in its religious significance or in the authority of those who worked in the temple; it did, however, mean that a primitive bureaucracy was in the process of creation, able to communicate its activities by reference to spiritual criteria, as well as perhaps by its monopoly of written records. The Sumerians envisaged the entire cosmos as a political entity: the natural forces which inspired them with awe were thought of as gods with full political rights in the cosmic assembly. Thus the highest in rank was the sky god Anu, joining with Enlil the god of the storm. Together Anu and Enlil embodied the two elements essential to human society: authority and the force to back it up. Just as one among the gods was highest in authority, so there could be only one king with supremacy, but each city or city-state was to have its own god and its own overlord.

In a few centuries in the second half of the fourth millennium, the scattered tribal societies of the Nile region became two well-organized monarchies, one for the delta and one for the upper reaches of the river. Then, in about 3000 BC, the two kingdoms were united in a single political system for the entire Nile basin. This was the essential condition for maintaining an economy dependent on the river, and the political and conceptual arrangements of the Egyptians reinforced it. Duality was to run throughout Egyptian history and pose a perennial threat to the stability of government, and indeed to the permanence of civilization itself. Kingship, which signified the unity of Egyptian life, was believed to have come into being at the time of creation. It was the necessary and abiding link between men and gods in sustaining the flow of the fertilizing waters and the management of their technology. The principle that had replaced chaos at the time of creation was the divine order both of nature and society, and therefore it also became the spirit of the justice which the king and his officials administered to his people. In offending against that principle, criminals and rebels were the creatures of chaos and were heading for their own destruction.

In Shang China the state was the family on a larger scale, the ruling house having access to unseen powers by virtue of royal ancestors who were gods to be approached by sacrifice and divination. The ruler himself combined his religious function as an augur with the economic functions of a chief landowner and the military functions of a war leader. His authority was subject only to the will of a supreme deity,

Shang Ti, who was liable to overwhelm the country with
storm and blight if the ruler failed in his duties and thereby
forfeited the right to rule. In Crete also, political and religious functions appear to have been combined in rulers who
also controlled the economic life of society, overseeing the
collection and distribution of food, raw materials and manufactures. Such evidence as there is for religious practices
suggests a close link between palace personnel and elaborate
religious ceremonies.

The Olmec state in Mesoamerica was dominated by a
hereditary class, which exercised judicial, military and religious powers and enjoyed favoured access to the best land.
In the Maya culture, the close links between political and
religious functions were apparent in the earliest writings,
which were concerned with portents and prophecies and with
legitimizing the authority of the rulers. The entire Mesoamerican world has been seen as a single system in which elite
level communication was the principal mechanism for maintaining beliefs and distributing material resources. Thus the
significance of self-sacrifice, ancestor veneration and funeral
rituals was familiar to members of the elite class in all
regions. As a consequence, the belief commitment remained
intact even when political boundaries changed markedly. The
interpretation of the moral order was in the hands of the
priests, but the sovereign and the nobility accepted sacred
tasks on behalf of the whole community. At the highest levels,
the priestly hierarchy and the leading administrative posts
were occupied by the same people.

The primary concern of all these societies, as they slowly
took possession of new areas of settlement, was to secure
their means of livelihood and make their situation permanent. The second and supportive concern was to find ways
of managing their common affairs so as to provide an acceptable degree of stability and security. The third was to
buttress these political arrangements with commonly held
beliefs related to their economic means of survival. The
physical configuration in which the civilized centres were
established showed considerable variation. Reflecting to

some extent these differences, they took on different features. But running through all the differences the political arrangements and conceptual patterns which underlay stability exhibited a remarkable convergence on common themes, outstanding among them the links between secular and spiritual and between local circumstances and universal principles. In all those societies, what had begun as ecological zones were acquiring an economic and political context and the elements of cultural communities.

Before moving on to the complexities of the civilized zones as their populations grew in size, it is worth asking why in their formative periods there were such similarities between them. The answer is that they all had to solve the same problem, the basic problem of feeding and equipping themselves and leaving something over for the future. Unless this could be done, and go on being done, there would be no future in that place to look forward to. No doubt there were failures and there was no future. The communities that survived were those that responded to the economic need and supported their response in the way they organized their affairs and shared their common purposes.

The primary concern

Part I has covered an enormous period (a hundred millennia) and an enormous territory (virtually five continents of the earth). It has also covered immense changes in the experiences of our species as they adapted to variations in climate and ecology. The most fundamental adaptations were from nomadic to settled existence, from simple sedentism to semi-permanent villages, and finally from groups of villages to civilized centres. Through all these transformations the primary concern was for subsistence, and in a succession of subsistence strategies, from foraging and hunting to cultivation, successful groups expanded with a consequent demand for more territory. In favoured regional centres greater productivity led to an economic surplus, more territorial expansion and more ambitious communal living.

As the settlements became more permanent and more prosperous there developed alongside the primary concern a range of problems as to how society should be organized. Even at the nomadic stage, group activity had led to some specialization and stratification in the drive for subsistence. As the settlements became more complex, as the communal tasks became more numerous and varied, the control and direction of group activity became more important. It was a precondition of stability that the political process was channelled along accepted lines of authority and that the authority was underpinned by commonly held beliefs. From one group of settlements to another, the patterns of authority and belief took different forms. Where they were successfully established and sustained, the achievements of what we recognize as civilized communities, or civilizations, were accomplished.

PART II
The Political Prospect

The need to protect the civilized centres, to prospect for raw materials and to trade with other communities led to more complex planning. Encounters with peoples living outside the centres raised the need for more extensive controls, military and administrative, and to attempts to build political empires. These, however, tended to be unstable and short-lived, until communications improved to the point of maintaining the authority of the core centres over the more peripheral areas. With the technological infrastructure of highways, alphabets and coinages, there also came a belief infrastructure to encourage loyalty to the wider ranging political systems. At their maximum extent the classical empires appeared to be responding to impulses of global dimensions, offering to diverse peoples the prospect of continuing well-being. In so doing, they were devising political superstructures above and beyond the ecological zones on which they had originally been based.

4

Hostile Encounters

The Threat from Outside

The constant movement of peoples which, by spreading knowledge of different techniques, had first contributed to the emergence of civilizations became later in the third millennium a threat to their stability. The growth of population which followed the exploitation of the alluvial soils, the inevitable extension into marginal areas less easy to cultivate, and the temptation to outsiders to help themselves to some of the riches of the settlements brought periods of confusion and uncertainty, threatening the permanence which had seemed to characterize civilization as a desirable way of life. The settled societies had indeed themselves been the source of some mobility in their search for raw materials, sending prospectors by land and sea to quarry stone, mine ores and fell standing timber. At the same time, the stimulus to trade over wider areas, the opportunities to herders to convert some of their wealth into agricultural land, and the movement of landless labourers, all contributed to a shifting of groups in a more or less continuous flux between core and periphery.

Beyond the patches of high culture represented by the literate settlements and the semi-permanent farming groups were tribes of mobile stockbreeders, ranging widely over steppe and semi-desert in search of pasture and the prospect of plunder. Over most of Europe and parts of Asia, peasant farming was still predominant. The methods of diffusion were various, by direct colonization of a new area, by a slow 'wave of advance' generation by generation, or by contact between hunter-gatherers and agriculturists whose techniques they learned to adopt because they were obviously more productive. Such contacts did not always, however, lead to the adoption of settled farming. A quite distinct way of life, more mature than the hunting economy, was that of the pastoral herders, which received a new spurt from the domestication of the horse as a pack animal.

As the ever mobile societies penetrated the areas of bronze manufacture and acquired more powerful weapons and tools, a fighting force began to grow on the northern periphery of the settled area from the Aegean to the Persian Gulf. At the end of the third millennium BC, there began a diffuse and eventually rapid movement of groups dominated by a warrior aristocracy of swordsmen and charioteers. Soon after the domestication of the horse, it was discovered that spirited stallions could be controlled by the use of the bit. The next step was to link the horse to the war chariot; and at about the same time the spoke was adopted for greater strength and lightness. As a fighting vehicle the chariot was drawn by two horses, with one man driving and another discharging missiles. This evolving combination of techniques gave a greater sense of freedom to the tribal nomads and a greater striking power when they encountered the centres of settled culture.

By the beginning of the second millennium BC, two contrasted global movements were at work in human affairs throughout Eurasia. On the one hand, there were the civilized centres, drawn for very practical reasons to extend the range of their authority, but carried further afield beyond strict necessity in response apparently to a more fundamental territorial or psychological drive. On the other hand, there were societies of growing military potential whose lifestyle was mobile, not from permanent centres but in a fluid relationship to land use. The extraordinarily wide spread of common linguistic elements among societies not necessarily linked in any other way is testimony to the overriding principle of unrestricted movement. Sooner or later, the outward

impulse from the civilized centres and the free-riding principle of the pastoralists were bound to come into collision;
and from 2000 BC it was a common occurrence. From the
destruction of civilized centres in central and south America,
a similar process of cause and effect may reasonably be
assumed.

Out of the confrontations between separate and different
ways of life, particularly at first in the Near East, there
emerged new political patterns to which, rather loosely, the
term 'empire' is often applied. Like 'civilization', the term
lacks precision; but its use signals unmistakably the arrival
of a distinctive phase in the evolution of human society. At
its loosest, the word is applied to almost any extension of
territory, any campaign of military conquest, any forcible
imposition of one people upon another. But more particularly it can mean the development of some centralized
authority, with the object of promoting some overriding
purpose, such as security or access to economic resources,
and requiring a technical support system based on improved
communications. Above all, perhaps, it can be seen as an
accommodation between the nomadic and the settled ways
of life, a political solution in effect to an insistent and widespread political problem.

Historians have tended to identify the first significant
attempt at an empire as the conquests of Sargon of Akkad,
after he had combined the middle and lower areas of the
Tigris–Euphrates basin and reduced city-state autonomy in a
bid for more centralized government over a wider territory.
If this was an empire, it was so as a military rather than a
permanent administrative accomplishment. The Akkadians
were apparently not themselves nomads; they lived in towns
and villages and practised agriculture, and they shared in
many ways the beliefs and culture of their neighbours downstream. So far as the city dwellers of Sumer were concerned,
the Akkadian intrusion was an invasion by speakers of a different language. What made this more than just a change
of rule, which in Mesopotamia was no new phenomenon,
was that after mastering the plain the Akkadians went on to

conquer the entire Tigris–Euphrates system and eventually extended their campaigning from south-west Persia to Syria and into Asia Minor. But the Akkadian empire, if such it is to be called, was short-lived, succumbing to a combination of internal rebellion and nomadic invasion. Every change of monarch seems to have been an occasion for unrest, and over the wider territories the rulers lacked the political authority and a technology of communications sufficient to sustain a genuine imperial system.

Military conquest was one thing: permanent occupation, let alone a continuous and stable administration of other peoples, was another. Armies of occupation had always to be fed, and rule through client elites was unreliable. Establishing a ruling-class ethos which was acceptable in all areas, together with the means of compelling social and economic cooperation, required a more mature political apparatus than was yet available. A notable innovation by Sargon's grandson Narim-Sin pointed perhaps in the right direction: he attempted to create a central rallying concept for widely diverse subjects by claiming for himself some attributes of divine status. The Akkadians had certainly given enormous prestige to the idea of empire, and others were to follow in the direction their aspirations had led them to take.

For a time the city of Ur was dominant in the delta, receiving tribute from provinces which stretched from the frontiers of Elam to the coasts of Lebanon. The Ur kings tackled some of the military and administrative problems which had defeated the Akkadians, using an efficient corps of messengers, for example, to keep themselves informed of provincial affairs and sending diplomatic representatives to other states; and their attention to the detail of bureaucracy seems to have been quite outstanding. But there were further invasions, this time from the east, and new city-state dynasties were established by the Amorites. This led importantly to a short-lived but notable pre-eminence of Babylon under Hammurabi, who provided a single code of law for the whole region in the first half of the eighteenth century BC. He certainly regarded himself as heir to the Akkadian empire and its aspirations, but he failed to leave an enduring state. In his lifetime, Babylon became a religious centre as well as the seat of kingship, and it gave a syllabic form to cuneiform script, enabling a single sign to have many different meanings or pronunciations.

But the apparatus for a full imperial system was not yet in place, and there were to be more examples of rule by warrior nomads before mature empires became a reality. The renewal of large-scale migration during the second millennium BC brought drastic changes in the political patterns of areas where civilizations had formerly enjoyed long periods of relative security. Egypt, Mesopotamia, India and Greece were all overrun; and settled societies faced the need to learn the techniques of the invaders to survive into a new phase of experience.

Some of the intruders belonged to the linguistic group known as Indo-European, who in the previous millennium had shared elements of language in an area stretching from south and south-west Asia across most of Europe. The likely cradle of this group of peoples was in the region of the Black and Caspian seas sometime before 2000 BC. Dependence on domesticated herds enforced a migratory way of life because the herds tended to eat grass faster than it could grow. An expansion east of the Urals would have taken the herders into steppe regions more sparsely populated, where their numbers increased to the point that their speech patterns were in use over the whole of southern Siberia. Their expansion would have brought improved access to goods, status, ritual practices, and ultimately security, for peoples still tied to particular areas.

Egypt fell for some centuries to the Hyksos people, who were of mixed Semitic and Indo-European antecedents. Their chariots gave them supremacy in the Nile valley until the Egyptians adopted similar techniques to repel them. With an improved weaponry, they then went over to the attack, and in the period of their New Kingdom they undertook several imperialist ventures. Beginning in the time of the six 'warrior kings', they subdued parts of Palestine and Syria, penetrating as far as the Euphrates, they campaigned against the Libyans in the delta region, and in the south they recovered Nubia. At about the same time, the military leaders of the Kassites, who are thought to have had Indo-European contacts, held political power in Babylon, where they worshipped the horse and probably invented boundary stones.

The collapse of the Harappan civilization, also at about this time, was accompanied and followed by tribal movements in the north of the subcontinent by peoples in the Aryan group of Indo-European languages, and it is accepted that the two series of happenings were connected. It is possible that as invaders the Aryans were to blame for the collapse; an alternative assumption is that they profited from it to establish a measure of dominance over Indian society. Their culture was not comparable to Harappan at its peak, but the newcomers may have assimilated some of its features and carried them into the Ganges basin, which became the centre of an iron age development after 1000 BC in a series of transformations which formed the basis of later Indian civilization.

Intrusive bronze age cultures of Indo-European association were also appearing in Anatolia and Greece. In Anatolia there seems to have been some systematic destruction of entire townships, sometimes by burning, and speakers of Hittite languages were becoming prominent. The petty kingdoms of the Mycenaean period seem to have been at war with each other, or in armed neutrality, expressing their power in lavish burial chambers and palace fortresses. Armed increasingly with bronze weapons, this loose confederacy of tribes was dominated by a military class, with a middle class of tradesmen and herders and a large supporting class of serfs. Iron was in use sporadically soon after 1500 BC and the Hittites were reputedly the first people with a steady local supply of the ore.

Some historians have used the word 'empire' in relation to the Mycenaean and Hittite conquests, though usually with some qualification. It is possible that some Mycenaean kings received tribute in the Aegean, and the Hittites at one time pushed their armies towards the head waters of the Tigris and set up some vassal states in Syria. They also had a legal system of their own and an open syllabary, but they were overthrown by other belligerent migrants around 1200 BC, leaving a vacuum of authority filled by Mycenaean kings until their strongholds fell to a new wave in the preclassical age of the Greek mainland.

A millennium or so after the hostile encounters across Eurasia, similar trends were appearing in the Americas. The widely extended Olmec culture, based on the cities of San Lorenzo and La Venta in the isthmus to the east of Mexico, was subject to constant threats of intrusion in the prevailing north–south movement of peoples. San Lorenzo fell to invaders around 900 BC, and half a millennium later La Venta was abandoned after being violently destroyed. Many of its massive monuments had been deliberately wrecked. Several causes for these happenings have been suggested. Expansion far beyond the central Olmec territory would have made enemies and left exposed positions. The great wealth of La Venta was undoubtedly an attraction. Olmec cities never recovered from these disasters. Mesoamerica remained an area of restless populations until more powerful empires were created.

In the Andean region, shifting populations and hierarchies were common factors over the centuries as old empires fell and new ones arose. The Chavin culture bore some resemblances to the Olmec, but direct diffusion from that source is now considered unlikely. The Chavin style spread widely in the northern coasts and mountain areas, possibly inspired by a dynamic religious impulse. The expansive period culminated with the abrupt disappearance of Chavin features and their replacement by diverse local developments. The generally peaceful nature of Chavin settlements contrasts with more warlike traditions elsewhere – a combination which may well have contributed to the sudden and dramatic outcome.

In the Old World, where the sequence can be clearly appreciated, the hostile encounters threatened the very existence of settled life and much the same appears to have been true of the New World. What was lacking was a technological support system to turn temporary conquests and fleeting hegemonies into the substance of enduring empires – above all, means of transport and skills of communication of a new order of magnitude. These were to be provided by the Assyrians and the Greeks in the Old World and notably by the Incas of Peru and the Aztecs of Mexico in the New World. In the empires which resulted, on virtually a global pattern, belief systems also provided an essential support in both core and peripheral areas, creating cultural communities with the capacity to survive the lifespan of political structures.

5

Communication Network

Paths to Coexistence

Although widely separated in time and space, the civilized centres of Eurasia and the Americas all encountered periods of instability as rival communities and peoples on the move threatened settled lifestyles. Attempts to extend the areas under control were everywhere a common response. But the difficulties of administering more distant domains were a recurrent weakness which only more effective means of access and communication could offset. Among the specific responses were maintained highways, written lingua franca, systems of exchange, and common religious commitments. By the eighth century BC, such responses had appeared in the Old World and were spreading across the cultures, and they would appear independently also in the New World.

The need for wide-ranging and stable political structures had become apparent before the end of the second millennium BC, and the first requirement was a system of recognized routes between peoples, along which soldiers and emissaries, traders and officials could travel in greater security. The first people to provide such a system were the Assyrians, whose chosen homeland was in the same higher reaches of the Tigris where the first moves towards civilized life had been made some four thousand years earlier. This area had been part of the military conquest of the Akkadians and of administration by the kings of Ur and it was accustomed to changes of rule. By about 1800 BC three major cities were united into a single kingdom by the head of an Amorite clan.

Originally tent dwellers, the newcomers had been attracted by the prospect of good grazing and a permanent water supply. Several centuries later, their descendants had become prosperous corn farmers and regional traders, concerned to protect an enviable lifestyle from the fierce hill people to the north and west. So began the Assyrian expansion which was finally to reach from the Persian Gulf to Anatolia and to be sustained by an efficient system of rapid communication.

The main routes were officially recognized and were maintained with regular posting stages to ensure reliable traffic between the capital city and the local areas. It was claimed that there was no part of the Assyrian empire that could not send a message and receive an answer within a week. The Assyrians were certainly not deterred by the varied nature of the terrain they had to cross. When Tiglath Pileser in the twelfth century BC extended his rule to include the Hittite domains, he had an engineering corps to lay pontoon bridges and level the tracks for carts and siege engines. 'I took my chariots and warriors,' he recorded, 'and over the steep mountains and through their wearisome paths, I hewed a way with pickaxes of bronze, and I made passable a road.'

It is notable that he referred to pickaxes of bronze and not iron. Throughout the second millennium BC, copper and bronze were virtually the only metals available. Late in the millennium, iron was being smelted in Asia Minor, mainly for weapons, but exports were probably closely controlled by the Hittites, who enjoyed an early monopoly. Not until the ninth century BC was the metal available in enough quantity to supply daggers for the troops; and it was also from this time that iron was used to make armour for the soldiers and war horses, for helmets and for axes to clear the tracks.

The Assyrians not only led the way in the construction of imperial highways: they were also among the first to proclaim a god-given mission to govern the peoples they overran. Any opposition to the military might of their armies was construed as an offence against the Assyrian god Ashur, who 'overthrows all the disobedient' and 'scatters the wicked'. There is no suggestion in the evidence that Ashur claimed a universal role at the start of Assyrian expansion; rather this entered into the theology of the conquerors as their political goals were enlarged. Originating out of the need for security, the missionary motive served thereafter to maintain the political momentum, providing in mythic terms current at the time an explanation of what was happening and a justification for it.

The increasingly frequent encounters of different peoples had stressed the importance of written communications and given encouragement to attempts to simplify them. Ideographic writing suffered from the same basic disadvantage as pictographic systems in that it required more and more symbols to the point where it broke down under its own weight and the burden on human memory. Syllabic writing avoided this dilemma to some extent, but it still required many separate signs and could only serve one language. Experiments to overcome these problems led eventually to a consonantal alphabet of about twenty signs, and there were some Canaanite examples as early as the eighteenth century BC. In the great jostling of peoples and tongues which followed the improvements in transport, this approach was revived by the Phoenicians, who, as the premier trading people, had the strongest of commercial motives for wishing to communicate clearly and reliably with all their customers. In the eighth century BC, their system was adopted by the Greeks as the basis for their alphabet, thereby creating the conditions for widespread literacy.

Early in the first millennium BC, learning from the people they had conquered, the new inhabitants of mainland Greece had themselves become mariners, exploring first the Aegean and subsequently the shores of the Black Sea and the Mediterranean as far as Spain. They laid the foundations of navigation by the stars and began making maps; and it was in their wanderings that they encountered the seagoing peoples of Syria and Palestine, and particularly the Phoenicians. After a period of continuous prosperity, the Phoenicians had suffered a setback, both from military invasion of their homeland and from commercial rivals; and it was then that the Greeks began their own remarkable experiment in colonization. Overflowing their city-state bases between 800 and 500 BC, they sent groups of settlers to mix with local peoples in a chain of new city-state communities. From this initiative arose cultures which acquired a common Greekness while retaining local traditions.

The Greek world had then the motive and the opportunity to complete the technology which the empires needed. The ruler of a small state in western Anatolia named Croesus introduced the first true coins in the form of pieces of metal stamped and guaranteed in weight and purity by a political authority. During the seventh century BC, the practice was adopted by virtually all the Greek cities as they issued their own bronze and silver currency; and the practice spread rapidly through other parts of the civilized world. Underlying the development was the increasing skill of metallurgists in excluding impurities and improving devices for accurate weighing. The consequent creation of a monetary system that was acceptable in different societies was the means both of expanding trade and of enforcing fiscal systems over wider areas.

By the fifth century, Athens had become the leader of a maritime league, devised at first as a protection but acquiring some of the characteristics of an imperial system based on Athenian ships and Athenian money. To give their ships the mastery of the seas, they built lighter craft for speed and ease of manoeuvre; and they financed the enterprise with silver mined from the richest seams in Greece. The urbanized coasts were controlled by means of monetary tribute: at its height the Athenian network comprised 150 cities, all paying cash into the central treasury. As well as financing the operations of the fleet, the tribute paid for some of the Athenian temples, adding thereby to the prestige of the city. The Athenian fleet reached its greatest power on the resources of the trading empire, but was reduced in conflicts with the rival cities of Sparta and Corinth. The Greek experiment in commercial and naval enterprise was permanently weakened as a result, but it had laid the foundations for a cultural community whose influences were to extend worldwide.

To a remarkable degree, and with no notion of what had happened in the Old World two or three thousand years earlier, the Incas of Peru in the fifteenth century AD laid a technological foundation for an imperial system in the New World. Expanding rapidly from a central site at Cuzco, they made conquests first to the north and then to the south. Following the same logic as the Assyrians, they created a system of main roads with lodges and supply bases along which their armies could move quickly and easily, improvising bridges as they went and building fortresses or fortified towns. To administer this vastly extended domain, they superimposed their Quecha language, which became the basis of government from the centre and communication between the provinces.

In Mexico, the Aztecs went some distance along the same path. Within the Valley of Mexico, the centre of the Aztec empire, a network of roads joined the principal towns and there were long-distance trade routes along which villages were responsible for upkeep and rest houses were provided. Trading missions were treated almost like small armies, equipped for battle in case trade was refused and required in any case to hunt out and report any military weaknesses. There were regular relays of runners, some carrying official letters from and to the capital. The Nahua language was used throughout the empire and the presence of Nahua words in local languages testifies to large-scale movement of peoples. As in Peru, trade was mostly in barter form, but some commodities served as currency: cocoa beans for small change, gold dust for more costly items.

In both regions the political impulse to expand was accompanied by a spiritual impulse to safeguard future society. The Aztecs believed that they had a divine mission to prevent the destruction of the earth, averting the death of the sun by human sacrifice as the apex of their penitential commitment. A large professional priesthood was maintained in the service of the gods and for the instruction of the nobility in an ascetic philosophical ideology. The Inca ruling family sought to weld their strung-out domains together by a complete control of their historical traditions, absorbing local beliefs into the state religion and using fear as the final social mechanism to secure conformity and sustain the Inca family in power. Like the Aztecs they accepted and enforced a mystical vision of a global role.

The political problem of coexistence between peoples – and most crucially between permanent settlements and intrusive nomads – was faced in many parts of the Old World, and over two millennia later in the New World, in attempts to create larger cohesive societies. While this in itself is significant enough in demonstrating a global impulse, what is yet more remarkable is the similarity of the networks of communication that were devised across the Old World and in the New World to make such larger cohesive societies possible. Once again, political and economic factors were at work in a complex interrelationship. In the Old World, the new technology prepared the way for the more powerful global impulses of the Persians, the Greeks and the Romans; and in the New World for the expansive tendencies of the Incas and the Aztecs, until a later generation of Old World empire builders overwhelmed them.

6

Global Response

The Spreading of Empires

The political imperative was now dominant across the linked societies of Eurasia. An empire covering the greater part of the known ancient world was created by the rulers of a Persian clan in the sixth century BC; and for two centuries it remained intact in their hands. It extended from the Aegean to India. It passed into the hands of Alexander the Great and his successors in an attempt to combine Greek and Oriental kingdoms in a single world system, founding Greek cities and spreading Persian influences as far as a native Indian empire. After his early death, Alexander's world empire became a group of rival satrapies in which the Greek language nourished a single cultural continuum. Centuries later, most of this Hellenistic system was absorbed piecemeal into a Roman imperial system which gave political unity to an area that encompassed north Africa and reached as far as the Atlantic. At about the same time, the Han dynasty united the separate kingdoms of China and extended civil administration into central Asia, Korea and the north of Vietnam. All these global impulses were sustained by the new techniques of communication, currency and control.

The Persian empire arose in consequence of an intense rivalry between military powers in west Asia which had led to widespread dislocation. The founder of the empire, the Iranian Cyrus, commanded a tribal confederacy which was partly sedentary and partly nomadic. His campaigns in Mesopotamia brought in a large population of skilled arti-

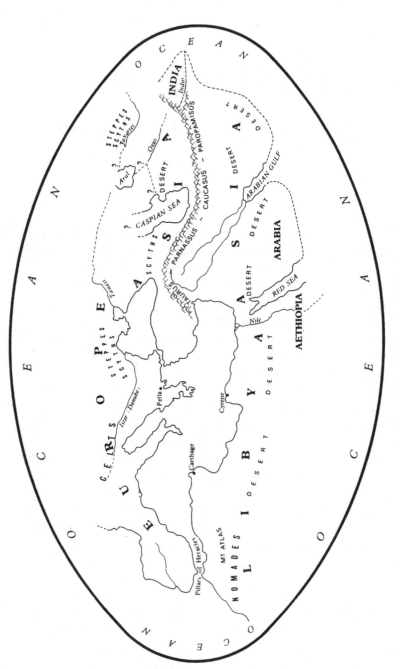

The world of Alexander (327 BC)

Source: N.G.L. Hammond, *The Genius of Alexander the Great*, Duckworth, 1997, p. 126.

sans and cultivators. Cyrus and his successors used all the devices of the communications revolution: their Achaemenian rule was the first complete example of what became a universal model. Under the direction of the later king, Darius the Great, it extended from the Mediterranean to the Indian Ocean, recruiting from the local populations of widely diverse areas some key subordinate officials, who became representatives of regional cultures as well as of the imperial power, imposing over and above customary local law the idea of a universal law.

The Persians knew about roads from the Assyrians and became the first rulers after them to create a permanent system and provide it with regular support, using bridges, cuttings and embankments, and providing staging posts where lodging and refreshment could be obtained by traders and imperial agents. Policed by imperial armies, the road system linked together people of distant countries sharing many common factors of daily life. This was the first society to use two precious metals as the basis for a world currency. The Achaemenians established an official relationship between their issues and those of the Greek states, eventually driving the latter off the market. They also adopted the Aramaic alphabet and it became the language of trade and administration throughout the empire.

In the fourth century BC the Persian armies were overcome by Alexander, with the possibility of an empire embracing Persians and Greeks in a still wider association of the known world. His initial aim in invading the Persian realm was ostensibly to exact retribution and partly to liberate Greeks in Asia Minor from Persian rule. As he penetrated deeper into Asia, he favoured the notion of turning the nomads there into peaceful cultivators. According to Plutarch, the leading biographer of the classical world, drawing probably on the words of Aristobulus, Alexander had a personal vision of the unity of mankind:

> Believing that he had come from the gods to be a governor and reconciler of the universe, and using force of arms against those

whom he did not bring together by the light of reason, he har-
nessed all resources to one and the same end, mixing as it were
in a loving-cup the lives, manners, marriages and customs
of men. He ordered them all to regard the inhabited earth as
their fatherland and his armed forces as their stronghold and
defence.[1]

To that end he respected the beliefs, customs and economies
of all the peoples he subdued.

Alexander and his successors took over the Persian road
system, establishing stations on the caravan routes and
garrison posts on the expanding frontiers. Links with the
west were reinforced by the foundation of new cities in
Asia to which large numbers of Greeks were transplanted.
Trade was stimulated in the wake of conquest, particularly
when Alexander released the Persian royal bullion into the
exchange system of the region; and with the wider circulation of Greek coins the Attic monetary standard was generalized throughout the Hellenistic world. Greek alphabets had
been spreading during the colonial period, and from the
beginning of the fourth century the Ionic form was adopted
by all Greeks, displacing other systems and becoming not
only the vehicle but also a means of creating Hellenic culture.
The political unity of the empire survived only briefly after
the death of Alexander, but the wide cultural continuum
remained. The enduring element was the Greekness of the
new cities. They continued to be ruled by a Greek minority,
committed to Greek institutions of government, religion and
education, and enjoying freedom of movement in what was
in effect one world.

Slowly the Hellenistic world fell under the control of
Rome, a city already under Greek influence when its expansion in Italy began. In the closing years of the republic Rome
enclosed the Mediterranean and began to reach out towards
the Atlantic. The Roman generals saw themselves as continuing Alexander's project for a conquest of the world. The
elite classes did not doubt that they were part of the same
Mediterranean civilization as the Greeks: indeed some were

fanciful enough to attempt to prove that Romans were Greeks. Their culture certainly was deeply influenced by the connection: they shared some of the same gods, they adopted the same art forms, and they based their literature on Greek models. The more robust Romans, it is true, had reservations about the softness of the Greeks and regarded themselves as abler soldiers and politicians. But the Hellenization of Rome was sufficient to enable its upper classes to cooperate with the leaders of the Greek world.

The foundations of three centuries of peace and prosperity were laid by Augustus. Ending thirteen years of civil war, he imposed a personal autocracy. He extended the frontiers to a point he deemed would be permanent; and he provided a solid structure from which developed a single administrative system, not only for the varied lands of the Mediterranean but also for much of northern and western Europe as well. The empire reached its fullest extent with Trajan's campaigns in the Middle East in the second century AD and the frontiers were consolidated by his successor Hadrian. It was to owe its enduring strength to two basic characteristics: the military genius of Rome and the Greek genius for building cities. These provided the framework, together with an infrastructure of roads, official stamped coinage and common languages, plus a judicious use of local autonomy.

The local magistrates, provided they maintained sufficient Roman standards and remained loyal to the empire, enjoyed considerable licence. The official incorporation of the provincial cities and the subject peoples within the Roman system gave them the security of Roman strength and Roman law, while encouraging them to apply local resources to public health, economic activities, and provision for leisure. Often with great generosity and civic pride, the local aristocracies undertook the building of aqueducts and public baths, temples and theatres; they maintained the city streets and the peace of the countryside; and they distributed grain and oil from the public supplies. The Roman system has been seen in its heyday as a wide confederation of prosperous and enlightened city-states.

Linking together the city communities and the structure of military command were the roads, first built for the Italian possessions and providing eventually a comprehensive arterial network for all the provinces. No natural barrier checked for long the progress of the Roman road-builders, as they mastered and traversed mountain and marsh, river and forest. The imperial currency served a primarily political purpose: to assert the personality and power of the reigning emperor, and to convey through inscriptions a range of propaganda on official themes. The first portrait to appear on their coins was that of Julius Caesar. After some currency crises, Augustus issued new coins in all metals which appeared abundantly in the western provinces, serving the needs of the army and administrators as well as commerce. Trade was never a major concern, but the Augustan peace brought conditions throughout the Mediterranean and beyond in which goods could travel more easily and diverse peoples could enjoy stable periods of prosperity.

The empire of Alexander also left a knowledge of the imperial idea with a local ruler in India named Chandragupta Maurya. He had come from the frontier area to seize Magadha, one of the more important kingdoms which had been created in the Ganges basin out of a fusion of elements from the Indus civilization and the nomadic peoples who had overrun it. These kingdoms had by the seventh century BC something approaching cultural unity in northern India, imposing Aryan religious ideas and a system of castes in an attempt to resolve the relationship of warrior aristocrats and peasant farmers. But politically this was an area of loose and disorganized rule, with the tribal units frequently in conflict and exposed to the threat of raiding across the north-west frontier.

To the extent that Alexander's campaign swept away numerous petty states, it helped to open the way for unification by an Indian dynasty. The Magadha kingdom, which in the fourth century commanded the Ganges trade route, was converted by Chandragupta and his grandson Asoka into the nucleus of the first Indian empire, the Mauryan, which was to cover all but the extreme south of the subcontinent. Inspired perhaps in part by the Persian empire, which under Darius had reached the Indian ocean, and more directly by the career of Alexander, the Mauryans perceived the merits of a wide-ranging political order. They created an elaborate administrative structure which included the recruitment of local rulers as provincial governors.

Here too the technological preconditions of empire had been met. Nearly two centuries before Asoka, there were Greek and Persian coins in circulation, and the earliest Indian coins known as punch-marked made their appearance during the Mauryan period. The Brahmi script, parent of all Indian writing, was superseding Kharosthi and was the earliest Indian script known to have been used for the writing of Sanskrit and Prakrit, both of which were employed by Asoka to communicate with his subjects. Finally the road system, already used by Buddhist pilgrims in the fifth century BC, was developed for commercial purposes and eventually covered the full extent of the empire, crossing the great forest belt of central India and serving the main ports. Asoka planted banyan trees to give shade and had wells dug and rest houses built every nine miles.

In China meanwhile, after the centuries of civil war which followed the Shang and Chou periods, the Ch'in dynasty attempted to restore some unity of government and made moves towards uniformity of administration. The script was standardized into something very similar to modern Chinese writing and local variations were eliminated; and from this time there were no further changes in the internal structure of the Chinese characters. The coinage was unified, together with weights and measures; and a network of tree-lined roads radiated from the capital. There was some attempt at colonization towards the unknown territories of the far south; and in the north the Ch'in constructed an enormous defensive wall to mark the dividing zone between the agricultural provinces and the steppe country peopled by horse-riding herders.

Ch'in administration was heavy-handed and their extended rule was unpopular and short-lived. Most of the elements for a more enduring system were present, however, and the process was completed by the Han emperors, notably Wu-Ti between 141 and 87 BC. Believing that the Han had reached a peak of achievement that should be recorded for posterity, his leading historian Ssu-ma Ch'ien attempted a definitive history of the Chinese past. Adopting a longer timespan than any previous work, and incorporating the affairs of foreign peoples, he reduced to an orderly narrative the complex events recorded in often contradictory sources, showing what was happening in each of the states at the same time. His treatment became the model against which all later histories would be measured. But Ssu-ma Ch'ien did more than research and record history, he also became involved in it by coming to the defence of a disgraced general. For this he was accused of defaming the emperor, which was a capital offence. Pleading to be allowed to live, he requested a reprieve so that he could finish his history. This was granted and he was castrated instead of executed.

In a determined military and administrative programme, the Han emperors were able to secure the northern frontiers against nomads, to establish colonies in central Asia and parts of Vietnam and Korea, and to assert the primacy of Chinese arms across the northern steppes. The chief threat to stability came from this source, but the Hsiung-nu tribal federations there were intrinsically weak: a system of vassalage was set up in the Han period, enabling mutually beneficial trading to be carried on. The road network was improved, and an efficient postal system ensured regular communication between the centre and the provinces. The main routes across the Great Wall were put in order and divided into stretches with regular stations. The minting of coin became a government responsibility under the Han, and the state currency gave a stability to trade which lasted until the end of the dynasty. With a brief interval early in the first century AD, there were Han rulers based on north China from 206 BC to

AD 220 in an empire broadly contemporary with the Pax Romana in the west.

From Sargon of Akkad and the first recognizable attempt at a political empire to the final death throes of the later empires of Rome and Persia, a period of thirty centuries elapsed. In virtually all this long stretch of time, there were nearly always empires coming or going somewhere in the vast geographical extent of Eurasia. On the narrowest view they may be seen as political responses to the political problems faced by all the civilized centres in their relations with other communities. On a wider view, they may be seen as showing the interaction of economic and political factors in the crucial contribution of technological innovation to the network of communication by means of roads, coins and alphabets. Impressive as this was in terms of sheer physical achievement, the outcome of the global impulse did not end there.

Before seeing how the creeds of empire sought in their own way to sustain conformity and allegiance, it may be asked why the imperial system was adopted by civilized societies across the globe and why it prevailed for so long. The answer is that they all resolved in a similar way a problem that would not go away, the problem of how to organize themselves and relate to other societies. In particular there were societies that were still mobile, sustaining themselves across the pastures and eventually (and not always peacefully) disrupting the lives and living styles of the settlers. In reconciling the political needs of nomads and urbanized peoples, the empires enabled them to live together.

The human species had also come to terms by the first millennium BC with disease-producing parasites, which had presumably occupied new ecological niches as a result of human disturbance of natural patterns. All the civilized regions of Eurasia had experienced some instability on this account, and the ebb and flow of peoples and empires no doubt increased the risk of epidemics. The balance between parasites and their human hosts was, however, sufficient to allow population growth and territorial expansion in the Mediterranean,

India and China. Early in the next millennium movement across central Asia and the Indian Ocean upset the balance to the extent that disastrous outbreaks of disease afflicted Mediterranean and probably Chinese populations, contributing to the economic and political breakdown of traditional society and a consequent loss of nerve. The transcendentalism of Indian religion at that time may also have been linked to conditions of poverty and disease among the peasantry.

The political prospect

As the settlements became more permanent, new imperatives had arisen. To the primary concern of subsistence was added an increasing concern for security, to protect what had been achieved and provide a stable base for its enlargement. Systems of authority and commitment, which had sustained the economic need to provide a surplus over subsistence, now dominated the political prospect as questions of status and hierarchy and the relationship of civil and military and religious leadership became more insistent. While such issues as these were thrust to the fore, others no less insistent arose in relation to external groups, some pursuing pastoral and nomadic lifestyles, some prospecting for raw materials and providing avenues of trade. These were basically political problems and they required political solutions. Expanding societies learnt from each other and from the intrusive warrior peoples, and slowly political techniques were adopted to give greater and more lasting security.

Political solutions in themselves were not enough, however, and there were renewed periods of confusion until they were given the backing of economic innovation. The acceptance of official standardized coinages made possible an essential financial control over wider areas while sustaining greater trade. In the service of commerce and administration, more secure networks of military roads were provided, and along the networks communication between peoples was enhanced by the invention and extended use of improved systems of writing. These were essentially technological innovations, which arose in the context of economic requirements and became crucially important in sustaining the evolution of political system. A common feature of all the empires was the official recognition of religious belief systems, which served initially to increase loyalty to the political structures, and in the spreading of the empires would eventually acquire global aspirations of their own.

NOTE

1 In N.G.L. Hammond, *The Genius of Alexander the Great*, North Carolina Press, 1997.

PART III
The Religious Factor

During the expansive phase of empire building, the ruling elites selected from available religious doctrines those which favoured social conformity and an allegiance by the peripheral societies to the authority of the centres. In this way, Zoroastrianism in Persia, Buddhism in India, the teaching of Confucius in China, and eventually Christianity in the Roman empire, were officially adopted in support of the political regime. By responding in their own way to impulses of global dimensions, the favoured creeds tended to overflow political frontiers and reach into other regions, where they encountered indigenous beliefs. As the political societies ran into limitations on their growth, they began to manipulate the belief patterns to help withstand loss of cohesion, contributing thereby to the divisions which were appearing in the belief patterns themselves, as new channels of persuasion were adopted for the approved orthodoxies. While the empires and their successor states continued to respond to the political initiative, they were increasingly subject to a spiritual initiative, which was at first enlisted for their support but in the process created independent cultural communities.

7

Creeds of Empire

Conformity and Allegiance

In the comparative study of religions, some merit has been seen in the idea of an Axial Age, a period between 800 BC and AD 300 when the beginnings of world religions were created in what was called 'a summons to boundless communion'. The period was certainly marked by seminal statements, in all the Old World civilizations, which recognized a global impulse towards common spiritual goals. The statements, which were generally made early in the move from civilized centres towards empires, were later adopted and given prominence by rulers who saw in them the social and spiritual equivalent of the tools of empire, a means of enlisting and sustaining support for their wide-ranging political systems. In time, the creeds were to become independent of political structures and some overran political boundaries as conflicting versions continued to serve political purposes.

The Achaemenian rulers of the Persian empire made three assertions in their proclamations: that they were the rulers of many peoples; that they ruled by the authority of the one true god; and that their rule was based on righteousness. Cyrus honoured the gods of all the societies he conquered, but he followed an earlier tradition in giving primacy to the gods of Babylon. Darius too acknowledged all the gods, but in the first place he put the Persian god Ahura Mazda, whose prophet Zoroaster had preached in Khorasan next door to the province where the father of the future emperor had been governor. He had to contend at first with revolts in several of the provinces. When he had defeated them and claimed his right to rule, he asserted the authority of Ahura Mazda in his support. On a rock face on the road to Babylon, he depicted the rebels with an inscription which told of their defeat. The main inscription then read:

> By the will of Ahura Mazda am I king, on me did Ahura Mazda bestow the kingdom. Ahura Mazda created me and made me king. Such was Ahura Mazda's will: he chose me a man, out of the whole earth, and made me king of the whole earth. Whatever I did, I did in accordance with his will.

Darius equated rebellion with what Zoroaster had called the Lie. By this he meant the denial of the spirit of good as against the forces of evil personified by his opponent, the dark god Ahriman. For the king, as for the prophet, the Lie was transgression of good order, the order of rectitude, of peace and prosperity. Rebellion was a violation of an order divinely appointed, and it was therefore the will of Ahura Mazda that the rebels should be dealt with according to the full force of the civil power. Here was the vital link between earthly authority and the will of the supreme god. Good was equated with loyalty to the secular power, evil with disloyalty.

In the Indian empire of the Mauryans, the chosen instrument for spiritual harmony and political cooperation was the teaching of Guatama the Buddha, which had acquired a following in the unsettled Ganges societies during the previous century or so. Unlike other itinerant holy men in the India of the sixth century BC, the Buddhists had developed a regular institutional life. Their basic unit was the sangha, a group devoted to full-time meditation, drawing support from their own locality but in touch with groups of monks in other areas. They had an interest in promoting a stable society as a background for undisturbed monastic life, and they welcomed a readiness to regard their rites and principles as a kind of social cement. The basic teaching was addressed to all castes and this was the most social of religions. The rulers were not blamed for the miseries of existence, which were attributed to the 'wheel of suffering'. Right conduct provided an escape for individuals who behaved with social compassion.

Without Asoka as their imperial patron, however, the Buddhists in India could have remained an obscure sect. They were in fact already splitting into numerous smaller bodies when the emperor adopted their teaching and proclaimed it along the imperial roads. The Mauryan empire was the outcome of a consolidation of smaller units. It needed a principle of wider citizenship which Buddhism (unlike Brahmanism, with its obsession with caste) was able to provide. India also had a tradition of a benevolent universal ruler known as the 'cakravartin'. The concept may have been somewhat shadowy before the Mauryan period, but the political needs of Asoka and the spiritual dispositions of the Buddhists combined to make it real. It has also been suggested that in the early stages Buddhism was supported by the commercial class because of its doctrine of social equality. The strength of the dynasty was heavily dependent on the growth of trade, so this too would have inclined the palace and the sangha towards making common cause.

The concept of 'dharma' – the universal law of righteousness as expressed in social and religious order – has been variously claimed as the political invention of Asoka, the spiritual creation of the Buddha, and the timely resurrection of the old Hindu concept of 'rita'. Whatever may be the truth of this, the basic principle served the needs of the times well. It was acceptable to any caste and to any sect and it was aimed at an attitude of mind favourable to tolerance and social responsibility. On one rock inscription, Asoka urged his subjects 'not to extol one's own sect or disparage that of another . . . Concord is to be commended so that men may hear one another's principles.' Buddhism also commended non-violence, an admirable civic virtue.

Just as the ideas of Zoroaster were revived and adopted
by the Persian emperors, and those of the Buddha by the
Indian emperors, so the ideas of Confucius were revived and
adopted by the Han emperors in China. In the preceding
period of the warring states, they had been given expression
by Mencius, who was both a philosopher and an official. He
taught that the state existed as a moral institution in its own
right and was carrying out a moral task. In one passage of
advice to rulers, he listed some of the imperial duties to be
discharged in relation to trade and communications, adding
that 'such a ruler will have no enemies anywhere in the
world, and having no enemies in the world he will be an
official appointed by heaven.' His contemporary, Hsun-tzu,
argued that without propriety and righteousness there would
be rebellion, disorder and chaos.

By degrees Confucianism came to play a central political
role as the official teaching of the Han dynasty. While the
emperor retained the right to use violence to enforce his
policies, the Confucian bureaucracy emphasized the need to
rule by moral example. The resulting amalgam has been recognized by scholars as Imperial Confucianism. It was given
official recognition in 126 BC when the first state university
was founded 'to transmit the sacred ways of the ancient
rulers and to achieve the moral and intellectual advancement
of the empire'. This development has been ascribed to Tung
Chung-shu, who combined his studies with political service
as chief minister. He taught that, because men are born with
greed as well as with humanity, they require a king to instruct
them; and scholars have seen in this proposition the main
reason for the choice of Confucianism by emperors who
needed an intellectual sanction. Tung went on to argue the
traditional case that the emperor could continue to rule only
as long as he retained the will of heaven. A rival school of
philosophy, the Legalists, exerted a considerable practical
influence. They emphasized the power of the state rather
than the welfare of the people, calling for the abolition of
independent political parties and a use of fixed bureaucratic
procedures. The Han governments, while declaring their

reliance on the Confucianist concepts of righteousness and propriety, showed some willingness to back them up with legalist measures.

The creeds to which the imperialists of Persia, India and China gave preference and prominence had all been in existence for some time. They were not devised, as it were, in response to the needs of the times; rather they were chosen from the religious traditions already available, with such additions and amendments as seemed politic to their new patrons. Zoroaster, according to repute, flourished in the seventh and sixth centuries BC, more than a century before he was extolled by Darius. The founder of Buddhism lived in the fifth and sixth centuries BC, more than a century before Asoka embraced his teachings as the official doctrine of his empire. Confucius lived at about the same time: his ideas were revived by Mencius in the fourth century BC and adopted by the Han emperors in subsequent centuries. None of these creeds was left unchanged in the process. Thus Zoroaster's original ideas were radically altered by the Persian rulers, Asoka transformed the obscure Buddhist cult into a universal social ethic, the doctrines of Confucius were amended by the Han philosophers, and centuries later the Roman emperors selected and attempted to enforce one version of Christianity. Before the Christian church was recognized by Constantine and given important legal rights, it had been much divided into a multiplicity of groups.

The motives in all these societies were political; but in the process the spiritual process underwent a profound change. The idea of an overarching religious authority or spiritual reality, matching the secular power of the empires, had taken root. It was through the wide publicity given to them by the rulers, who controlled all the channels of communication, that the visions of some outstanding religious thinkers in the first millennium BC became familiar. As the empires ran into administrative problems, the influence of the religious movements which had been recruited to support them increased and became more pervasive. In the early centuries of the first millennium AD there was a widespread process of assimilation of religious ideas across the civilizations in a profound and enduring manifestation of the global impulse.

8

Crossing Frontiers

Faiths and Universalism

The process by which local cults became aspirants to regional religious leadership, and ultimately to roles of more universal significance, was intimately bound up with the global political impulse. When the cohesion of the empires weakened, and they lost the capacity to reassure their subjects, the ideologies lingered on, acquiring independent identities. Moving freely across more open frontiers, often along routes opened up by traders, they offered to confused and uncertain peoples a prospect of consolation. From being the official sanction of ruling elites, they became the personal religions of ordinary people. Slowly but steadily the spiritual dimension moved away from the political dimension to acquire an ethos and an authority of its own. The prevailing response to the challenges of decline and fall became, over the centuries, less and less a matter of command structures and more and more a matter of faith and hope.

The empires had attempted a task of heroic complexity. Their aim had been to bring within a single system of government peoples of diverse customs and traditions, deploying over vast areas new techniques of communication and administration. The remarkable thing is not that in the end they failed, but that for a long time they succeeded. To many generations they had brought peace and the opportunity to reach standards of unprecedented well-being, with periods of high intellectual and artistic achievement. The simplest explanation of their eventual breakdown could be that they attempted too much in responding to a global impulse and could not sustain what they had created.

The Achaemenian empire failed, not so much because Alexander set out to avenge the Greeks, but because he envisaged the still more ambitious project of world dominion through a combination of Greek and Persian culture. In India, Asoka had perhaps asked too much by calling for adherence to a law of righteousness and non-violence in societies riven by differences of sect, caste and economic interest; and the Gupta empire, in an attempted renascence, was to lack the effective central control of the Mauryans, facing its own internal economic troubles as well as the intrusion of the Huns. In China, the Han empire had grown too much and too rapidly, its many philosophies only half-digested, and neither its political strength nor its cultural base was sufficient to sustain a system so extended. The Roman empire, perhaps the most impressive of them all, received an apt epitaph from Gibbon: 'the stupendous fabric yielded to the pressure of its own weight.'

Throughout the period of the classical empires, the same basic themes occurred again and again. One, perhaps the main one, was the difficulty of sustaining effective control from the centre. The second, to some extent associated with it, was the lack or loss of commitment to the centre from the parts of the empire. The third was the failure to resolve peacefully the confrontations with other empires or would-be empire builders. The fourth, which overlapped with the third, was how to accommodate intrusive forces of nomads. The improvement over the period in the technology of transport and communications, and the growth of commitment to supportive ideologies, equipped the rulers for a time to deal with the first two problems. But the onset of one or both of the external problems with one or both of the internal weaknesses was generally fatal.

During all these shifts in political circumstances, people everywhere continued as far as they were able to produce and trade, and when political relationships broke down goods and services continued to flow along the channels they had opened up, not least along the ancient silk roads which crossed Asia. The great trading systems of the Mediterranean and the Middle East, of China and India, and the lands and oceans around them, had built up networks which did not disappear when the political core–periphery nexus failed. Where trade links persisted, there were always channels along which religious movements could travel. Where officials and soldiers of empire had been carriers of approved doctrines, the monks and itinerant holy men of more troubled times could find willing listeners in societies still hopeful of harmony.

The central Asians themselves ranged from pure nomadic habit to sedentary societies which built cities and practised metallurgy, facilitating movement across the borders with the civilized regions of China, India and the Middle East. The commodities transported included ceramics, glass, precious metal and gems, and there were also other long and middle-distance land routes, as well as sea routes linking south and east Asia with Africa and the Mediterranean. For a time the Chinese controlled the central Asian route. The empires of Han China and Rome, although they lacked diplomatic contact, were linked in the second century AD by commercial contact, for which the Indian Kushan empire and the Persian Parthian empire provided support by garrisoning the roads.

Zoroastrianism, the first of the creeds to be adopted by empires, infiltrated neighbouring societies in a variety of guises. This ancient religion already had common elements with religious traditions in India, and in its Zoroastrian form it would easily assimilate in the subcontinent. More significantly for the future of world religions, it influenced the Jews during the Babylonian exiles in the sixth century BC. The antithesis of good and evil was taken over by the prophets and reformulated in a god who was exclusively good and an antagonist who was the author of evil. Absorbed then into Christian thinking, this duality spread through the Roman world, where the Persian deities of Anahita and Mithras were

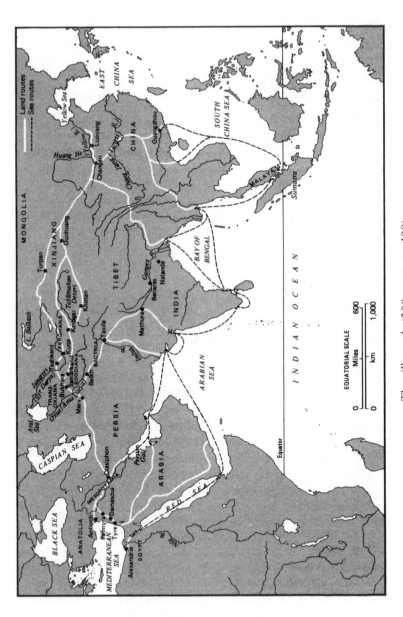

The silk roads (200 BC to AD 400)

Source: J.H. Bentley, *Old World Encounters*, Oxford University Press, 1993, p. 34.

also widely popular and at one time appeared to challenge the appeal of Christianity.

Weakened in its country of origin by the campaigns of Alexander, and by destructive rival cults in a later Persian empire, Zoroastrianism as such never became a world religion; but it entered indelibly into the spiritual global impulse. It entered prominently into Manichaeism which became one of the most pervasive missionary religions in the third century AD. Its Babylonian prophet Mani absorbed the ascetic tradition of Christianity in a syncretic system intended to appeal to the whole world. Despite persecution, it became rapidly established from the Middle East to Spain, as well as in Egypt and north Africa, and was to find a home in central Asia and China, assimilating to Buddhism and Taoism.

Competing creeds from a variety of sources flooded into the Roman empire alongside the prevailing worship of the state and its emperors, aided and abetted by the administration of distant areas. Roman officials and soldiers on frontier duty encountered different religious ideas and practices and sometimes converted to them. From Egypt came the still lively cult of Isis. There was in this something of the universalist idea prevalent in all the empires, together with the feminine attraction of the Nile goddess and some promise of immortality in the hereafter. Mithras made a stronger masculine image, perhaps as an ally of the all-powerful Egyptian sun-god. He entered Rome from Asia Minor and there he absorbed some elements of Greek religion and might have aspired to become all things to all men. But the exclusion of women, the absence of priests and an apparent lack of tenderness ruled out a fully universalist role. Christianity, free from these particular handicaps, can be seen in retrospect as the more likely candidate.

Appearing in one sense as a fulfilment of Hebrew scriptures, with its concept of the supreme godhead, in another as reflecting the cosmic conflict of good and evil central to Zoroastrianism, Christianity also had resemblances to the mystery religions of Greece and Rome. Its main strength in times of political uncertainty was the belief in a saviour god who was in some sense identified with the supreme ruler of the universe, seen in the new testament more as a god of love than as the wielder of retributive justice. Offering concern and comfort for all peoples who believed, the Christian apostles and their successors survived the trials of persecution and imperial vacillation to infiltrate Roman society from below.

The Christians were also challenged by a movement of synthesis subsequently designated as Gnosticism, from the Greek word for secret knowledge. This group of doctrines, prominent throughout the Roman world of the second century AD, drew on Platonic as well as Egyptian and Mesopotamian sources in offering an escape from the material world, regarded as basically evil, through the pure life of the spirit. In countering its influence, the Christian theologians emphasized the essential goodness of the created world, the redemptive suffering and death of their saviour, and the importance of personal moral regeneration. More important perhaps for the survival of the Christian communities and a strengthening of their influence was their organization by pastors and bishops and their readiness to accept the burden of social responsibility in conditions of political instability. In this respect, they offered some parallel with the progress of Buddhism at the other end of the civilized world.

From the Indian subcontinent, both Buddhism and Hinduism travelled abroad on the trading networks. Central Asia was profoundly influenced by Indian culture, primarily Buddhist but also Hindu. The people of that region adopted Indian scripts and language and some art forms as well as the two religions. While Buddhism became the dominant religion in Burma and Sri Lanka, Hinduism prevailed in much of south-east Asia, and the norms of Indian society such as the caste system were widely adopted. On the island of Sumatra, the Hindu kingdom of Srivijava lasted from the fourth to the seventh century, and in Java there were Brahmanical temples, prominently those dedicated to Vishnu and Shiva. Contacts between India and the west were mainly on the material plane, but they also provided a channel for religious and intellectual influences.

The Mauryan emperor Asoka sent Buddhist missionaries to the Hellenistic kingdoms and into south-east Asia. The religion was also carried through Afghanistan into central Asia and eventually reached the western frontiers of China. It was here that its influence grew rapidly and eventually collided with the traditional strongholds of Confucianism. In the process, it was able to exploit a number of analogies with native beliefs. Tribal incursions into northern China created conditions favourable to the absorption of Buddhism. It was adopted by the invaders to consolidate their conquests and became a source of comfort to the common people. In the breakdown of society which followed the collapse of the Han empire, Buddhism penetrated more widely, helped by the development of a more appealing version which allowed the salvation of many more adherents through enlightened intermediaries who delayed their own entry into nirvana to perform pious deeds on their behalf.

Although some Chinese intellectuals were attracted by the novelty and freshness of Buddhism, which contrasted with the more prescriptive quality of Confucianism, the official doctrine never lost its pervasiveness and its grip on the ruling classes. Its links with the procedures and prerogatives of power ensured that, when Chinese rule was extended into wider areas, it was sanctioned by Confucianist rubrics. As such, it was an element in the Chinese penetration of Japanese culture, and it was to remain a powerful and abiding tradition throughout East Asia.

The phenomenon of religions leaving their countries of origin, crossing political frontiers and becoming established in regions of different spiritual orientation has to be related to what was virtually a universal search for unifying principles across the civilized world of Eurasia. Over some thirty centuries, political expansiveness had enlarged the human vision. At all times, it was accompanied by supportive patterns of belief appropriate to regional circumstances. What has since been recognized as a flowering of religious thought in all regions assumed a universalist character which outlived its period of origin. In particular, it survived through the centuries in which the empires encountered limitations on their growth, experienced internal weaknesses and lost control of their frontiers.

By their very nature, however, the migrations of religions across frontiers reflected the divisiveness of political rule, partly because they were manipulated for political reasons and partly because the confrontations between creeds were themselves an inevitable source of dissension. In the next chapter, the divisiveness of doctrine is shown as a prelude to the eventual twilight of the classical world.

9

Division and Decline

Propaganda for Salvation

As the structure of the last political empires of the classical world came under strain, attention was turned increasingly to religious doctrines; and there began an intense rivalry between contending ideologies. Selected versions were given the authority both of holy writ and political endorsement. In new instruments of persuasion, they were circulated in permanent form and proclaimed in sacred buildings of awesome appearance. In what were the main technological advances of the age, the printed word and its proclamation were adopted alongside official approval. The emphasis on orthodoxy, and the sometimes harsh repression of alternative versions and creeds, may be seen as a recognition that plurality of belief was a source of weakness in the apparatus of faith and in the ailing political systems in which it was still embodied. In a crisis of belief across the continents, the period of assured classical culture was drawing to a close. In the final wars between the civilizations and their challengers, and in the massive migrations which followed, the universalist religions were the best hope of individuals and at the same time the surviving carriers of the global impulse.

In the political and social crises at the end of the Han dynasty, the traditional Confucianist doctrines were modified by Taoist mysticism on the one hand and authoritarian legalism on the other. To many, there appeared little choice between anarchy and dictatorship. The revival of legalist theories was expressed in demands for the state to be strengthened by penal measures indifferent to ancient rights and privileges. The mass appeal of Taoism, and of Buddhism, which was at first regarded as a variant of Taoism, was part of the reaction. During the next few centuries, China became in effect the land of three doctrines, all competing with each other and seeking the patronage of would-be successors of the Han dynasty. Buddhism, despite its otherworldly aspirations, became well organized and embarked on a power struggle with the official classes.

Meanwhile, the teachers of the rival doctrines made innovative use of new techniques of communication: these included paper and printing, and religious art and architecture. The official canon of Confucian writings had been drawn up early in the Han period, together with the correct interpretations as approved by scholars, and it was decided to perpetuate them in a more permanent medium. To this end, the authorized texts of the 'five classics' were engraved on stone tablets and placed in the imperial college in the capital. Confucian scholars had also exploited the discovery that paper could be made from various raw materials. It was cheaper than silk and lighter than bamboo, and its use facilitated developments in calligraphy. So Confucianist ideas were disseminated more widely, using for example block printing to engrave religious texts and pictures for the instruction of pilgrims. At the beginning of the fourth century, Taoist scholars collected and published religious and alchemical works and their propaganda gained them more influence at some of the northern courts. The Buddhist scholars had begun to adapt Indian texts from the second century, and by AD 200 they were translating on a considerable scale. It is thought that, apart from the difficulty of rendering Indian meaning into Chinese, there was deliberate modification to make the ideas more acceptable, for example by allowing prayers to be offered for departed ancestors.

For five centuries after the decline of the Mauryan empire, the Indian subcontinent was fragmented politically and subject to invasion from central Asia. For a time, Buddhist thought and habit had been the main surviving influences from the first age of Indian imperialism. Monastic institutions flourished, with alms from lay believers, while monks and nuns strove zealously towards nirvana along the eightfold path. Some of the monasteries attracted such considerable endowments that they were able to employ slaves to do the work. The hope of salvation in an uncertain world also gave Hinduism a new strength at this time. Two main forms emerged, focused on the gods Vishnu and Shiva: both called for the emotional devotion of the believer, leading respectively to contemplation of the god and eventual identification. In an accompanying philosophical speculation, various systems of observance were introduced: among them was yoga, which aimed at the complete quiescence of all functions of the mind and caused the soul to return to primitive inactivity.

When the north was reunited by the Guptas, the myths and images of both Hindu and Buddhist thought were expressed in vigorous artistic form and were at once a vehicle for the Indian national spirit and a philosophy of universal appeal. The great Indian religious epics, the Mahabharata and the Ramahana, were put into definitive form as the official documents of the Gupta kingdom. Originally secular sagas, they were adapted by the Brahmins to give popular reinforcement to priestly admonitions. Into the Mahabharata, which celebrated the heroes of the Indian past, they introduced the Bhagavad-Gita, the gist of which was that a man should do his duty according to his caste and his stage of life.

The characteristic elements of the Hindu temple emerged in the Gupta age and continued long after its decline to proclaim the transcendence of religion. At the heart of the design was a sanctuary which housed the image of the god. Immediately above was the highest point of the structure, the symbolic mountain peak. The axis between the two signified the ascent of the human to the divine. It provided the main stimulus in the development of building techniques to create complex superstructures culminating in soaring towers.

Whole companies of skilled artisans toured the country from one temple project to another. Funded by monarchs and merchants, they were the main constructional undertakings of the age and the clearest evidence of its universalist aspirations.

The Buddhists had carved their earliest chapels out of the hillsides around Bombay, using the very substance of the earth to emphasize the permanence of their law. The basic pattern was a central nave for services and a space for contemplation. The image of the Buddha was universally popular, embellishing old caves and new; and, as the worship of images was extended, the temples were built to accommodate them. The characteristic stupa was a commemorative monument to house sacred relics and texts and to symbolize the elevation of the Buddha. The literary output of the Indian Buddhists was vast but is almost impossible to date. For at least four centuries the tradition was transmitted orally across Asia, but it was certainly in writing by the Gupta age when the Chinese were making translations.

After the breakdown of the first Persian empire, the unity of the Iranian peoples was destroyed and the Zoroastrian religion lost its privileged position. For a century and a half most of the Iranian lands were ruled by the Seleucid successors of Alexander and became subject to the influence of the Greek elements in the cities. A native Iranian dynasty, the Parthian Arcacids, became powerful for a time, their hopes of empire checked however by the ambitions of Rome. The Euphrates became a political and spiritual frontier between the west Asian civilization and the Mediterranean. Early in the third century, relations changed when a new dynasty, the Sasanian, set out to restore the previous Zoroastrian-based regime. Its founders came from an area where these traditions had been preserved; and when in power they turned the association to political advantage, believing that religious commitment could bring together their mixed ethnic elements and provide a common focus of loyalty.

During the reign of Ardashir, the architect of the new empire, the scattered writings of the doctrine were brought

together and given the status of official approval. A campaign
to exterminate rival cults and creeds was proclaimed. The
political need of the regime was essentially to maintain the
power of the centre against the interests of the great families
who ruled in the satrapies. In offsetting their influence, the
weight of the priesthood was needed behind the dynasty, and
the promotion of the state religion was a necessary aspect
of imperial authority. The state was divided into ecclesiastical districts, with a hierarchy of clergy whose head was
appointed by the emperor. Special buildings were set up in
the localities to house the sacred books alongside legal documents such as title deeds and archives. Imposing temples were
built, sometimes in the style of royal palaces to echo their
authority, as in the important town of Bishapur where a great
temple was consecrated to the central fire ritual.

Almost from the beginning, the regime was in rivalry with
Rome, and both civilizations were threatened by barbarian
forces from Asia. Against this unsettled background, open
hostility often flared between Zoroastrian and Christian
adherents. In the fourth century, Shapur persecuted the Christians in his domain during a military campaign against the
rival empire. When peace was restored some toleration was
shown towards the Christians, but they were thought to have
abused the privilege and persecution returned. In the fifth
century, when the empire was on the brink of economic
disaster and threatened by barbarians, there was further
disruption from a communist Mazdakite movement.

In the fourth century, the centre of Roman government
was moved to a new site in the east and Constantine converted the state to Christianity, believing that its universalist
aims would help to unite conflicting peoples and classes.
Theodosius defended the frontiers and held society together
at the cost of harsh regimentation under the adopted creed.
An edict promulgated in 380 denounced as 'heretical and
mad' all who declined the description of catholic Christians,
and condemned them to suffer both divine punishment and
'the vengeance of that power which we, by celestial authority, have assumed'. At a time of competing interpretations

of the faith, Theodosius accepted the Nicene creed as orthodox and rejected all others, embarking on a systematic programme to abolish them together with the many pagan rites and religions circulating in the empire. Believing that he had found an effective principle of political cohesion, he announced a series of measures to enforce uniformity of belief.

It was at about this time that the Christian authorities began to make effective use of the available instruments of propaganda; and it was in respect of the word of God and the houses of God that the most notable technological advances of the age were made. Following the example of the Jews, whose sacred writings they adopted as their old testament, the Christians assembled their own canonical writings in an approved new testament. To give it wider currency, they used the new codex in preference to rolls of papyrus and wax tablets. Consisting of written pages stitched together, the codex was the earliest form of manuscript. It eliminated cumbersome unrolling and re-rolling and could be conveniently consulted and cited in public. Whereas a papyrus might contain only a single gospel, a parchment codex could offer the whole testament in one volume. By being in the same form as the law books of the late Roman empire, they also acquired authority by association.

The oldest extant biblical codices in Greek date from the fourth and fifth centuries, and it was at this time that the Christians started their great programme of church building. Here, too, by association they sought to echo the authority of the Roman state, using as their model the basilicas which housed the law courts. In the manner of Roman judges facing litigants, the bishops and presbyters sat facing their congregations. The central mystery of the religion, the holy communion, was performed at a table set between priest and people. Unlike the pagan rituals, however, in which the worshippers were commonly spectators, the Christian services required congregations to participate in the mystery.

As the spiritual imperative overtook the political imperative of the empires, it received the support both of the political authority and of the latest technological innovations. The sacred canons of the universalist churches, and the sacred buildings dedicated to their proclamation, survived the demise of the classical empires, carrying into a new world the message that the unity of faith was still possible despite political collapse. During centuries in which the splintering of authority was accompanied by a decline in living standards, the spiritual imperative was sustained, bequeathing its own forms of government and pastoral care.

The crisis of faith which characterized the early centuries of the first Christian millennium was felt just as acutely across all the expiring empires. Where to look for security (indeed for salvation) as the political structures crumbled? The creeds which had sustained the empires in their heyday had not expired with them. Moreover they had shown a remarkable capacity to overrun their frontiers in a spiritual aspiration to globalism. In a renewal of widespread migration in which the remnants of civilized life were first overwhelmed by the nomads and then absorbed into new patterns, the universal churches provided elements of social infrastructure to which new rulers could gratefully turn.

The religious factor

As the empires attempted larger and more complex political tasks, and drew on the innovations of financial cohesion and a greater security of trade, they found opportunities in religious practices to acquire ideological sanctions for political authority. Emerging often from local loyalties or earlier traditions, belief patterns which encouraged social conformity were enabled by official recognition to spread along the imperial roads and communicate through the writing systems. By becoming in effect the spiritual equivalent of the political infrastructure, they survived in periods when the empires faltered, and when the empires failed they gave a semblance of continuity not only in the imperial domains but reaching across still wider frontiers. In times of confusion they discovered their own sources of authority to combine communities of believers and offer succour where it was needed.

The belief patterns now became the dominant factor, drawing into their own ambit the surviving political processes and using for their promotion whatever advances in economic processes were available and appropriate. Outstanding among these were materials and methods to increase the reach and permanence of written records and to provide impressive structures where the approved doctrines could be expounded and approved rituals consecrated. Surviving political elites manoeuvred to participate in the content and the control of the now dominant ideological factor. As their rivalries came to be mirrored in the competing sects and schisms of the aspiring religious organizations, a mood of profound searching became endemic across the regions of fading imperial rule.

In the centuries following the crisis of belief the religious movements reorganized and regrouped under their own authority, strengthened by their core commitments as they assumed the care of their congregations and provided guidance and intellectual resources across the abandoned territories of the classical empires.

From Classical to Modern

This survey of the classical era has been constructed around the successive experiences of regional civilized societies, expanding political empires and would-be universalist churches. But how much justification is there for seeing the classical era as a part of global history? And what value is there in the grid of phases and factors in ordering the historical data? Part of the answer to the first question lies in the way the penetration of the global habitat set the scene for developments on a worldwide scale. Sedentism appeared independently at numerous sites, and villages became the norm of settled habitation. From this point the sequences of the settlements began to appear. In terms of the answer to the second question, the understanding of history in terms of the framework of phases and factors, it is apparent that from the beginning of the settlements the human experience centred around three basic community requirements: getting a living, working together and sharing ideas. All of these were always in play, sometimes one and sometimes another taking the lead.

In all the regions the belief factor became dominant. In western Europe the barbarians who succeeded the fall of Rome were converted to Christianity, their kingdoms and tribal domains becoming known collectively as parts of Christendom. The Byzantine half of the Roman empire survived on the basis of a concordat in which the clergy supported the state and in return controlled activity in

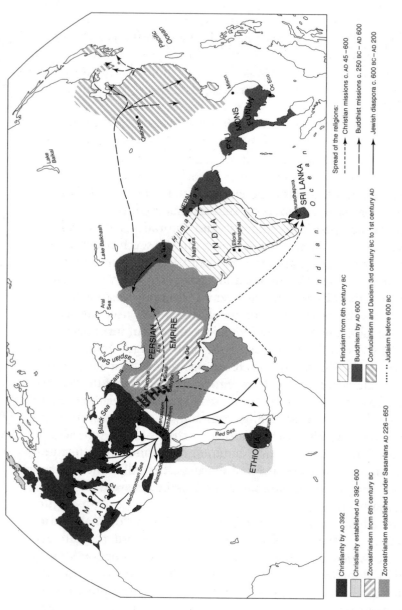

World religions (to AD 600)

Source: Based on *Philip's Atlas of World History*, George Philip, 1999, p. 44.

Constantinople and were accorded status throughout Christendom. In Persia the last imperial regime, the Sasanian, survived when nationalism was imbued with Zoroastrian fervour. Under the last imperial regime in India, the Gupta, Hindu culture reached its highest peak in a cultural renascence. In a politically severed China the feature common to north and south was the progressive spread of Buddhism.

The centuries after AD 500 were characterized in the Old World by the extension of organized religion, confused and continuing movements of population, shifting and short-lived political regimes and localized subsistence economies. Christendom became increasingly identified with Europe in separate eastern and western traditions, Buddhism flourished particularly in areas of ideological plurality such as China, south-east Asia and Japan, and from the seventh century the forces of Islam shared the Near and Middle East with traditional religions. While most of central Europe was settled by Slavs, the borders of the Byzantine empire fluctuated with varying campaigns in almost all directions, nomadic power formations shifted endlessly across and out of inner Asia, and from China the influence of the Tang spread along the Silk Road. In a constant ethnic interaction, piecemeal political groupings crystallized in Frankish western Europe, the Kievan state in Russia, Arab states from the Mediterranean to the Indian Ocean, Khmer kingdoms in south-east Asia and trading townships in west Africa.

In the Americas, too, there was a period of decline and attempted reorganization. The classic period in Mexico had been based on the supremacy of Teotihuacan and its trading and tribute empire. When the city fell in the seventh century the empire broke up into petty kingdoms. Political disruption also afflicted south America, where frontiers contracted and settlements were fortified. Recovery came in Mexico with the arrival of the Toltecs, a warrior people from the north, while in south America two separate and possibly antagonistic polities were based on the cities of Huari and Tiwanaku. The settlement at Huari was originally surrounded by extensive irrigation in a mountainous terrain, while Tiwanaku was supported by flatland cultivation in a lakeland area irrigated by long canals. The influence of the Maya kingdoms, which was widespread in Mesoamerica, collapsed in the ninth century with a major dispersal.

In western Europe after AD 500, patchy settlements tended to become overpopulated but with the growth of the Frankish kingdoms specialization and exchange increased. Further east the Slavs raised crops and animals around small unfortified villages, some using Roman ploughs and rotation. Across the steppe lands nomadic peoples moved their flocks between the summer uplands and lowland winter pasture. Bedouin tribes from Arabia exploited the fertile regions of the former Persian empire, and wheat became the staple cereal under the reign of the early Caliphs. In southern China new agricultural land was opened up by peasants in the early Tang period, and in south-east Asia rice irrigation was practised in the floodwaters of Angkor. In west Africa the forms of agriculture varied in different zones, from the cultivation of yams to pastoralism and herding. In Australia the aboriginals used a variety of techniques to harvest marine life, hunt kangaroos and emus, and hurl boomerangs into flights of birds.

In four of these areas soon after AD 800 subsistence was converted into surplus by agricultural innovation and the basis was laid for civilizing centres to grow. There was already a platform of economic practice on which peoples who had settled in favoured areas were able to build. Although land and water management had been neglected during the political upheavals, there was still a residue of techniques that could be recovered and developed in a comparatively short time. Much the same was true of political techniques, which could be carried into new areas, for example from the Mediterranean to western Europe, from the north of China to the south, and from Persia and Byzantium into the areas overrun by the Arabs. Modified to fit new circumstances in different habitats, the political practices of the classical era were easily absorbed into the practice of the modern era.

In the next part the centuries of movement and settlement in which this came about are described, from agricultural advances in new regions to the search for wider identities. The interregional patterns of exchange, which had never been wholly abandoned, eventually became absorbed into modern world systems.

THE MODERN ERA

PART IV
New Beginnings

For several centuries from the decline of the classical empires, the movement of peoples was resumed on a massive scale as the civilized centres from China to Europe were overrun. By the ninth century there were new ethnic blends in areas from the Pacific to the Atlantic and around the rim of the Mediterranean, exploring the habitats for what became the early modern centres of civilization. Four in particular found the resources to produce economic surpluses: by means of agricultural revolutions in southern China, Islam and western Europe; and in Russia from a run of improved harvests combined with extensive trade. In support of the primary economic thrust and its technological innovations, alliances were formed in all four regions between the political and spiritual elites. In China the Confucian scholars, in Islam the successors of the Prophet, in Russia the Orthodox church and in western Europe the Catholic church gave sanction to the secular search for wealth and power.

10

Movement of Peoples

Nomads and New Settlers

The political equilibrium of the civilizations which has been perceived by some historians in the first two centuries of the Christian era came increasingly under strain in the third and fourth centuries; and there is a consensus that in the fifth century the crisis of the classical world reached a peak, marking the end of one phase of history and the beginning of another. The cause of the crisis, it is often said, was the massive movements of mounted nomadic peoples across Eurasia which overwhelmed all the civilizations. Nomadic invasions were indeed a perennial factor, before, during and after the last days of empire. If, however, the fifth century was the turning point (and there are good reasons for thinking it was), then other factors than tribal intrusions must be taken into account. In particular, there was at that time a spiritual and intellectual crisis, a movement of deep anxiety across the whole civilized world, as the classical empires appeared no longer to be able to guarantee political security and stability.

Religious yearning and philosophical speculation were certainly not confined to the fifth century, but there was at that time a search of unprecedented vigour and marked eclecticism for new principles to guide the future course of mankind. It is significant that this search was undertaken, not independently of political developments, but closely involved with them. Roman, Persian and Indian emperors, and provincial rulers in Egypt and China, were all engaged in the inquiry and made pronouncements regarding it, as they appraised the value of competing faiths and ideologies to bind political societies that were falling apart. If the fifth century is to be accepted as marking the great divide, the universal spiritual crisis of the empires provides part of the explanation for the movements of nomadic tribes, who may be seen as taking advantage of the weaknesses of the civilizations rather than causing them. More significantly, the nomadic movements were a kind of reassertion of the global impulse, which several centuries later settled new peoples in what became the regions of new civilized centres, Chinese, Russian, western European, and eventually Islamic.

Unlike the speakers of the Indo-European languages who had overflowed in the second millennium BC, the newcomers used languages that were mostly of the Altaic group, associated with an area that extended from the north-eastern region of Asia into China, Siberia and the Middle East. Their primary centres of power were not in arid steppe or desert, but in the more favoured regions closer to China. From here they struck out in a series of movements. After being repelled or held at bay, they came to dominate northern China and caused large numbers of people there to migrate to the south. Meanwhile, a separate confederacy in central Asia was associated with movements which destroyed the Gupta empire, overran much of the Sasanian empire, and finally set in motion the movement of Germanic peoples who infiltrated the Roman empire. The links between all these peoples remain speculative, but the general pattern was of nomadic pastoralism and formidable mounted aggression.

There were also population movements at this time in parts of Australasia. Around AD 300 there appears to have been new activity throughout island Melanesia and western Polynesia as Samoans ventured eastwards in canoes as far as the Marquesas, which became a primary dispersal centre, sending settlers, foodstuffs and technology widely across the islands. New Zealand was reached but developed its own subsistence system as hunter-farmers settled in mainly coastal areas and experimented with new tool-kits in a distinctive

Maori culture. Groups in central Australia ranged over wide tracts of territory, but larger numbers were supported in smaller areas of the fertile river valleys and along the coasts, sustained by local plant and animal foods.

From the fifth century, the classical empires confronted the steppe peoples and each other in what might be characterized as the wars of the civilizations. There was intermittent war between Byzantine and Sasanian forces, and with the nomads who sought to take advantage of the conflicts between them. A campaign against the Huns in the late fifth century had in fact been a disaster, leaving the nomads the victors and the Persians contending with famine and fears of an apocalypse. From this numbing experience, they turned away towards the softer lands of Mesopotamia, where, in the sixth century, they found themselves confronting the forces of Byzantium. Seeking to recoup their losses at the expense of their western neighbours, they began to loot the area as a way out of bankruptcy. In an all-out counterattack, the Byzantine forces put the Persians into retreat and seized their most valued religious sanctuary. The entire Byzantine economy had been placed on a war footing in what was perhaps the first total war in history. All exploitable resources were mobilized for military ends and the currency was drastically adjusted to pay for the war effort. The Persian collapse was indeed total, but Byzantium too was exhausted by its supreme effort. Between what was left of the great empires lay ravaged lands and defenceless peoples.

The sequel was the last great war of the period and its most extensive, a world war in fact which carried the Arab armies to the western limits of the Roman world and to the frontiers of India and China. There are several ways of regarding the wars of the seventh century. For many historians, they decisively marked the division between antiquity and the interlude before the beginning of the modern age. For some, they have been seen as the last desperate struggle between competing political systems. For others, they were ideological encounters, the struggles between rival interpretations of the destiny of peoples on earth and their relations with their deities. Certainly it was seen in those terms by those who experienced the holocaust and sought to justify it to their followers.

By some twelve centuries ago, the world of the classical civilizations had passed. Everywhere peoples had been on the move, looking for new habitats. Mounted nomads had roved the plains of Asia and Europe, plundering the old urban centres and pushing other peoples aside. The security of the old frontiers had gone. Slowly new areas of settlement appeared, political order returned and systems of farming and trading were renewed. Four regions in particular were important in this process: western Europe, the river systems of the Russian steppes, the fertile areas of the Middle East, and the river and coastal basins of southern China. Here the seeds of new civilizations were to be sown. What are now recognized as revolutions in agriculture were important, not only in the context of subsistence, but for the creation of the surpluses without which permanent societies could not endure; and here the development of trade within and between them also played a crucial part. Over several centuries, commercial and industrial innovation contributed to the further development of the societies.

In all of them, tensions arose between secular rulers and the custodians of belief. The resolution of these tensions depended to a significant extent on the way the economic life of the communities had developed: in western Europe open and exploratory, allowing commercial and some intellectual freedom; in Russia by the exercise of monopoly control; in Islam by a wide response to market forces; and in China by the infiltration of commercial values into the bureaucracy. Everywhere, political forces and patterns of ideas responded to the need for stability and economic growth.

The peoples who formed the new western European societies arrived over several centuries in an area which faced towards the Atlantic. Much of the region to the west of the Rhine had been settled by Celtic peoples who were skilled metal-workers. East of the Rhine were various German tribes, primitive in comparison but beginning to farm and trade across uncertain frontiers. In the fifth century the area was disturbed by Hunnish peoples from central Asia. In the next century, a larger and steadier movement carried the Franks from their Rhineland base into northern France and Anglo-Saxons into England. Finally, beginning in the eighth century, came the Northmen, the Viking masters of the open seas. With the withdrawal of Roman political authority, the religious authority of Rome passed to the Christian bishops and presbyters. By 600 the Anglo-Saxons were being converted, and by 750 the faith was being carried to the Germans.

The Vikings had also undertaken mercantile ventures to the east, through the Baltic and into the river systems of Russia. Here they were to encounter some of the Slavic tribes from central Europe who had been displaced in the eighth century. On the trade routes along the Dnieper to the Black Sea and along the Volga to the Caspian, the Vikings helped to turn the Slavic settlements into fortress towns and forge trading links with the Mediterranean and the Middle East. The Kievan state there lasted from the ninth to the thirteenth century, and important Kievan traditions were transmitted to Russian civilization as it emerged from the Mongol occupation.

While the Vikings were exploring from the north into western Europe and into Russia, the Arabs were fanning out from their peninsula into all the lands of the Middle East. There was a longstanding tendency for desert bedouins to seek new pastures and in the seventh century the movement reached crisis proportions. Political and economic disturbances upset the balance at a time of rising population, and under the added stimulus of religious fervour they entered the borderlands between the east Roman and Persian empires which lay unprotected after the wars. Together with the skills of peoples already long settled in the region – Greeks, Syrians, Persians and Egyptians – the followers of the prophet Muhammad created the basis of Islamic civilization.

During much the same period, the formation of modern Chinese civilization was taking place to the south of the area of classical civilization. The centuries since the great Han dynasty had been filled with invasions and migrations. While the north was being occupied by Turkic and Mongolian cattlemen from the Asian steppes, emigré Chinese families were colonizing the indigenous peoples in the south and facilitating immigration from Vietnam, Cambodia and parts of India. In the early T'ang period, efforts were made to secure the northern frontier, but it was along the Yangtse and down the southern coast that the beginnings of the new China emerged under the Sung emperors.

During these centuries, other groups of people, nomads and primitive agriculturists, explored on a transitory basis the potentials of many and varied habitats across the Eurasian land mass. Some created tribal kingdoms for short periods, within or linked with the areas of the new civilizations, and between all regions trading communities were sustained by the wealth the civilizations were creating.

This sequence appeared independently in east and west Africa, leading by the tenth century to towns, trading networks and the beginning of nation states. In the sixth century a variety of subsistence strategies sustained different cultural groups in east Africa, ranging from foraging to stock-breeding, and by the eighth century more settled communities were engaged in trade. In west Africa there were important trade centres at that time which led eventually to urbanization and state formation. By the seventh century the earliest known African town was acting as an exchange market for savannah products, salt and metals. Ghana was probably the first state in west Africa, followed by a quickening of activity around Lake Chad. Nearer the coast the forest kingdom of Benin produced bronze sculpture, and nearby Ife was the birthplace of the mature Yoruba nation. By the ninth century trans-Saharan camel trade was being stimulated by the consolidation of Islam, and by the tenth century there were major trading networks across the northern half of the continent.

It is, however, with the four regions where settlements proved permanent that the following narrative is concerned:

in western Europe and in southern China following shifts from political to economic contexts; in Islam by the creation of an ecological zone from India to Spain; and in Russia by an eastward movement from Kiev to Moscow and beyond. Despite their differences, there was in all regions an initial process to provide subsistence and acquire a surplus; and the political and religious leaderships entered into supportive alliances.

11

Economic Breakthrough

New Bases of Subsistence

The end of Roman rule in the west had left a political vacuum and a cultural ruin, and as late as the ninth century the physical outlook was of a vast wilderness, with here and there clusters of occupation. From this low level began the struggles from which a new civilization arose. There came over the centuries a quickening of change, as higher productivity and surplus population began to fuel the assertive tendencies of a newly confident society. Feudalism was the political and economic base, emerging in the tenth century and reaching its zenith in the thirteenth century. The bedrock of the system was the entrenchment of the power of local aristocrats and landowners over the peasantry, who occupied and tilled the land but were not its owners. The estates were held as a fief from a superior noble who could demand military service in time of war and who in turn was the vassal of liege lords upwards towards the monarch.

During the four centuries of its existence the feudal system allowed for striking increases in agricultural productivity, which yielded the essential surplus to create permanent civilized centres. Land clearance intensified, and within two hundred years the forests which once covered most of central Europe had largely disappeared. In a major modification of the natural environment, ploughing advanced at the expense of woodland and marsh, with a widening belt of farmland around the settlements. Some later techniques undoubtedly owed something to eastern sources as well as to

Rome, but the craftspeople of western Europe often had little alternative but to find their own solutions to problems as they arose.

In the drive for territorial acquisition which seized society during the early Middle Ages, the manorial estates became the main matrix around which relationships could be organized. New equipment, such as plough teams and mills to grind the corn, was expensive and it was economic to install it only where there were enough people and an effective organization. Joint undertakings by the better-off peasant families were sometimes attempted, but the surpluses were generally raised through seigneurial revenues in the form of rent in money, labour or in kind. The early economic objective was the growing of grain, but a gradual rise in the living standards of the nobility introduced meat and wine, stimulating the growth of small market towns inhabited by dealers in these and other products.

From being at first centres of exchange, the towns also became centres of production, of cloth and clothing, footwear, leather and metal goods, and they attracted the crafts associated with building, such as brick-making, masonry and carpentry. There was an increase in the numbers following these occupations and they used craft guilds to protect their interests. The merchants and more important manufacturers founded companies to reduce competition and restrict entry. They had different interests from the lay and ecclesiastical lords and before long they were insisting on urban autonomy and claiming the right to make their own fiscal and juridical arrangements.

When the population continued to grow while yields on marginal or overworked land began to fall, the ecological balance of the system became increasingly precarious. In the fourteenth century the bubonic plague struck the population of the towns, leading to the collapse of production in many areas. There were poor harvests, famine and consequent neglect of the land. In what is known as the great crisis of Western European feudalism, uprisings of the peasantry spelt doom to the system and halted economic advance, until new patterns of social relations were established with help and stimulus from the towns.

Two regional groups of towns were particularly influential. In the Low Countries, land had been claimed from the sea by building dykes and polders; free of traditional restraints, the population grew rapidly and an early form of capitalism appeared. Loosely linked to the Low Countries through the Rhine valley, and soon cross-fertilizing with them, were the free cities of north and central Italy, with their enterprising merchants and bankers. The main international trade, in bulk and in prestige, was in woollen goods, and both the Dutch and the Italian towns prospered as commerce took to the sea. There were significant advances in seamanship – in flexible rigs and the introduction of the sternpost rudder – and the Italian commercial houses used double-entry bookkeeping, banking credit and the insurance of goods in transit. Such innovations spread into a trading network which also drew in the Baltic ports and the raw wool suppliers of Spain and England; and through the Mediterranean western Europe was linked into a wider intercontinental trade.

Classical Chinese civilization ended with the downfall of the Han dynasty, a few centuries before the end of the Roman empire in the west. Some centuries later, a new beginning was made. Whereas classical Chinese society had been based on the Hwang-ho river basin and was oriented towards the north, modern Chinese society arose in the Yangtze river basin in the south and drew the north into its sphere of influence only as and when the Chinese world was reunited. By that time, quite different people were involved, both in the south and in the north. In a striking parallel to developments in western Europe, the breakthrough began with an agricultural revolution, which opened the way to advance across a wide technological front. The introduction of wet rice cultivation, with new techniques for lifting and moving water and new tools for tilling, brought a dramatic increase in yield and released labour for commerce and manufacturing. Between the eighth and the twelfth centuries a vast economic transformation took place, spreading in time along the grand canal and major rivers to the northern ports.

Among the more striking industrial developments were the creation of a high-temperature iron and steel industry, based on coking coal and the use of metallurgical bellows, and the invention of textile machinery. The first known accurate mechanical clock was made in the eleventh century, at about the same time as the formula for gunpowder was discovered and movable type was used in printing. This was an exemplary literary age when encyclopaedias, inventories and collections of texts were published. Scientific inquiry was the source of exceptional progress in fields as varied as medicine, geography, mathematics and astronomy.

The towns grew in number and importance through the Sung period, both as commercial centres and as places of culture and entertainment. Merchants and craftsmen were brought together in corporations and guilds, and there were beneficial contacts between officials and the urban population. Paper money came into use to facilitate the flow of goods, together with cheques, promissory notes and bills of exchange. Trade grew rapidly within and between regions, and some large merchanting houses made their appearance. A coastline with good anchorages, linked with a network of internal waterways, encouraged the growth of seaborne traffic; and, with the help of the compass and other technical improvements, the southern Chinese ventured into long-distance voyages.

Between western Europe and southern China lay another region which, by the tenth century, was experiencing an agricultural revolution in the formative stage of a new civilization. Islam, the outcome of forces of economic and social change set moving by Arab conquests which began in the seventh century, arose in the core areas of much older civilizations in the Middle East and the Mediterranean. But the extensive urbanization and trading networks it generated owed less to that than to the merging of Arab and non-Arab peoples in a habitat favoured at that time by innovation in farming knowledge and practices.

Bedouins in search of pasture and caravaners in search of trade found there a plenitude of resources, which they exploited at the expense of the populations already living there, displacing or absorbing the former landowners. The new Arab rulers, occupying existing cities and creating some new ones, inherited a chain of commerce that linked the Mediterranean and the Indian Ocean in a potentially profitable complex. In new conditions of stable government, the production of crops was stimulated and new sources of food were introduced. Recent research has shown that, between 700 and 1100, the diffusion of crops and farming techniques over a wide and unified area laid the basis for a new and very different civilization. The productivity of the land and the labour force was raised through the introduction of higher yielding crops from Asia and better varieties of old crops, together with improved irrigation and intensive cropping and rotations. Many peoples contributed to this outcome, but it was the receptiveness of the Arabs, their mobility and their extensive commercial connections which provided a favourable medium for diffusion.

Irrigation systems which had been allowed to decay were restored and new ones were constructed, using a range of techniques to channel, store and lift water needed for summer cultivation in areas of scanty rainfall. Instead of long periods of fallow, there was multiple cropping, yielding for example several cereal harvests in a year, with heavy manuring to retain fertility. Cultivation was pushed even into steppe and savanna, and swamp lands were recovered for farming. By the tenth century, virtually all Islamic areas were watered sufficiently to receive the new crops.

Some of the towns were little more than local markets, others were centres for skilled craftspeople, and those near to a sea or river or caravan route became linked into the long-distance trade. While the stability of life continued, the larger cities came to be grouped in a great chain and, by the tenth and eleventh centuries, they were the largest in the western half of the world, stretching from southern Spain to northern India. They were centres for manufactures, too, supplying both the local demand for textiles, household appliances and processed foods, and the wider market for higher quality goods. Advances were made in glass manufacture, and when paper-making was introduced from China enough mills were set up to make paper a product of daily use.

The fourth region in which a new civilization was formed from the ninth century onwards was the mixed forest and steppe belt of western Russia. Conditions there were, however, far less favourable for sustained agricultural improvement than they were in western Europe, the Middle East and southern China. Exceptional circumstances did allow for some limited temporary gain, and shifting settlements pushed cultivation from the steppes into the forest. Here there were furs in abundance and other products for which there were markets in the still wealthy lands of the eastern Mediterranean, and, whereas the land gave little more than subsistence, it was trade with Byzantium which provided the margin for an economic surplus. The crucial factor that enabled this new society to achieve an economic take-off was a period of benign climatic conditions when a comparatively isolated area of fertile land was being occupied.

Because of the poverty of most of the soil and a generally unfavourable climate, early Russian agriculture afforded insufficient surpluses to nourish urban life. The peasants tended always to be shifting, for the slash-and-burn method caused soil exhaustion. But, in common with much of northern Europe, there was an improvement in the climate from about 800, leading to improved harvests, particularly from the tenth century. By then the Kievan state included an area to the north-east which, by a geographical anomaly, contained fertile black earth. This combination of circumstances enabled the Slavs to consolidate their position in their new land and made marginal farming a more viable risk. When the Vikings came, they had a keen interest in trade and soon identified the water-borne routes to the markets of Byzantium and the Middle East. Commercial openings there in the ninth and tenth centuries led the way into more sustainable growth. At its zenith around the year 1000, Kievan Russia was the largest state in the west and enjoying contacts throughout Europe.

In the twelfth century, however, there was a shift away from Kiev towards new urban centres to the north-east. To the ancient settlements of Suzdal and Rostov were added a new city and stronghold at Vladimir and the beginnings of Moscow. The land itself proved suitable for colonization and there were some improvements in ploughing, crop rotation and manuring. The river system allowed for more extended trade links, providing in particular easy portages to Novgorod and hence to the Baltic. The period from the thirteenth century, when Novgorod became a leading member of the Hanseatic League, was outstanding for Russia's involvement in international trade.

The particular strength of Moscow in economic terms, which enabled it to become the paramount city of the Slavs and eventually challenge and defeat the Mongols, was the geographical position which connected it with all the key river systems of northern and western Russia. The strategy of its princes was to gain political control. They turned energetically to trade wherever profits could be made and used the proceeds to acquire towns and territory. After subduing Novgorod and opening up a vast fur-bearing region from the Gulf of Finland to the Urals, they turned to the west to gather in all the Slavic lands, both in the 'great Russian' area traditionally linked with Moscow and in areas like the Ukraine which had formerly been part of the Kievan state.

From the new civilized centres – the free cities of north and central Italy and the thriving markets of the Low Countries, the Yangtse river basin and coast of southern China, the Arab settlements of the Middle East and along the southern rim of the Mediterranean, the Kievan state and its more successful successor in Muscovy – growth economies spread out across four main regions. Attempts have been made to link the trading systems of Europe, the Mediterranean, the Middle East and the Far East into the beginnings of an integrated system of exchange which in some sense anticipated a world system between 1250 and 1350. For a brief moment it might

have seemed that across Eurasia from the Atlantic to the
Pacific there stretched integrated spheres of commercial relations. But if to any extent this might have been true, by 1400
such a system had disintegrated. What had not disintegrated
was that the new civilized centres, in creating surpluses, had
provided the wherewithal for the early modern civilizations
to arise, and that after 1500 enduring contacts between them
would be made. By then the inherited traditions of religious
and secular rule had been modified in support of the primary
economic thrust as it drew on a heritage of tools and techniques from the classical world and created the potential for
further advance.

12

Church and State

Twin Pillars of Stability

Between 1000 and 1500, as the civilizations of western Europe, Russia, Islam and south China emerged, they were greatly exercised by questions of authority and faith. Religions came from outside into all four regions. Over partially converted kingdoms of the barbarian west, the Catholic bishops sought to exercise the authority of Roman Christianity. In Kievan Russia and its successor state of Muscovy, it was the Greek orthodox form that was adopted by the princes and given to the peoples. Into the region which was to provide the central homelands of Islam came tribes of militant Arabs, primed with the belief that they possessed the truth of religion in its final form. Buddhism had entered China from India and for a time became influential as an alternative to orthodox Confucianism. All the societies into which these religions came were obliged to come to terms with them and seek a workable relationship between them and the new forms of material and secular growth.

In Western Europe the issue of sovereignty, in Russia the issue of state monopoly, in Islam the political strains of a society of believers, and in China the role of the mandarins in a commercial society forced their way to the centre of developments as the civilizations assumed their definitive form. Christian Europe acknowledged both a spiritual and a secular creed as land-hungry conquerors proclaimed a different mission from that of otherworldly priests. In Russia the authority of religious leaders was subordinated to the autocracy of princes and tsars in a wide and baffling terrain. In a theoretically egalitarian Islam the powers and privileges of the state were modified and checked by the rules of the prophetic revelation. In China traditional wisdom was adapted to the needs of agricultural and industrial production. In these four widely different civilizations, rule and belief reacted and responded to the economic imperatives of subsistence and surplus.

The conversion of Europe to Christianity took place against the background of three processes: the arrival of successive waves of new peoples out of Asia, the withdrawal of Roman political authority, and the assumption by Christian bishops of the mantle of Rome in the new barbarian kingdoms. At first uniformity of ritual and even belief had been difficult to achieve. The missionaries were careful to adapt to particular regional needs, and between the Christian communities there was ample scope for differences of opinion. But by the fifth century the bishop in Rome had appeared to be the natural leader in a city of imperial tradition, using the cult of St Peter to secure devotion to his see. Among the sources of commitment to the Christian faith the religious orders were outstanding. Widely spaced throughout western Europe, dedicated communities were specially endowed to perform and proclaim the spiritual life, often in association with practical vocations such as farming and rural crafts. The influence of the monasteries extended far beyond their walls, and the security of kings and magnates depended crucially on their influence. In return they were increasingly endowed and were able in consequence to survive the vicissitudes of a changing society, contributing to the institutions of government and education in an economically progressive system.

From the eleventh century, the most usual term for western Europe was Christendom, which at first signified commitment to a set of beliefs, namely those of the western church, but increasingly signified a territorial entity. As such, it was associated with a group of ideas which included physical expansion, economic growth and assertive distinction from the rest of the world. This was not the Christendom of the Roman empire, but of a new western European civilization. While accepting the Christian story as preserved in its monasteries and preached in its churches, it accepted also the literature of conquest, a heroic story in its own right, equally fit for mythic treatment. As the new civilization developed in different ways from its predecessors and its contemporaries, it was inspired by both stories in a changing pattern of rule and belief. It was a very real alliance between the aristocracy and the church that led European society into a more self-consciously progressive understanding of itself and its capacities. Despite their different affirmations, they both showed by their actions their commitment to land, wealth and power.

From the power vested in the productivity of the land, in the material and spiritual authority of the church, in the financial independence of the towns and the intellectual independence of the universities, there emerged a complex of forces shaping the new society. Slowly, and with many checks and balances, came a concentration of powers which from the thirteenth century increasingly took the form of sovereignty. This had two main aspects: providing law and order within the territory, and defending it against attack. Both required armies, centralized administration and some system of taxation. In the three westerly kingdoms of England, Spain and France, it was the acceptance of a hereditary monarchy at the apex of the system which pointed the way forward. By the end of the century, royal supremacy was well established and a sense of nationhood was beginning to take hold. In the new climate of thought, less and less attention would be paid to theories of the supremacy of the priesthood, more and more to the realities of secular rule and commercial leverage.

The sequel to the end of feudalism was a shift towards a centralized and militarized state and an economic system known as mercantilism, or the rise of commercial capitalism. Reaching its mature form in the seventeenth and eighteenth centuries, the concentration of power in the hands of the ruler was later codified into a general theory of absolutism. The reality had never been as clear as the theory, but ruling houses buttressed by the estates of the realm sought by means of war, trade and diplomacy to exercise increasing power in international affairs. In this extremely competitive environment the beginnings of an international system took shape.

The Christian mould in which Europe had been enclosed since the fall of Rome was not yet broken, but the essence of rule for western Europeans was the wealth of land quickened by the wealth of trade, and whoever commanded that wealth was sovereign over priest and layman alike. A new ideology for a new Christendom substituted for the concept of earthly resignation the concept of historical progress and a glad acceptance of change and innovation. In France absolutism took the form of a hierarchical corporative society bound closely to the dynastic state and based on traditional orders and privileges. In the complex revolution which broke out there at the end of the eighteenth century, the *ancien régime* was destroyed. In its place powerful ideas were released into European (and eventually global) societies, prominent among them the creed of nationalism and the revolutionary doctrine of liberty, equality and fraternity. In its most potentially explosive form the French National Assembly proclaimed on 26 April 1789 that men were born and remained free and equal in rights and resistance to oppression, echoing the sentiments of the American Declaration of Rights in 1776 which had spelt out the nature of human rights which all men continued to enjoy when they had entered into a state of society.

From the foundation of the Kievan state in the ninth century, during the Mongol occupation in the thirteenth and in the rise to dominance of Moscow in the next two centuries, the links between church and state in Russia were crucial in holding society together and ensuring the survival of its basic economy. The newly emerging settlements had drawn the surplus for permanent institutions from trade with the still wealthy society of Byzantium. In converting their people to the orthodox Christianity of that society, the Kievan rulers provided them with a complete package (as reflected in the art and architecture of the four hundred churches of Kiev); and the church, in its turn, accepted and reinforced the state's authoritarian role in administering scattered populations over a wide area. The secular rulers of the Kievan state founded monasteries, built churches and granted a tithe to the clergy, requiring and empowering them to suppress paganism and preach social submission. The usefulness of the church in securing obedience was recognized by the Mongols, and they excused the clergy from conscription and taxation.

In the thirteenth and fourteenth centuries Mongol tribes from the depths of Asia responded to their own global impulse in a vast movement of primitive nomadic peoples stretching from Korea to the frontiers of Germany, from the Arctic to the Persian Gulf. In the process they dispersed Turkic tribes across western Asia, influenced the hold of the universalist churches of Buddhism, Islam and Christianity, and left a permanent mark on Chinese, Indian and Russian civilizations. As the Mongol empire disintegrated into separate states they acquired their own individual features. In Russia the independent power of the princedoms was destroyed, a general census of the population was taken and a taxation system was established.

During this period the church played a vital role in holding Russian society together and sustaining its trading links with the outside world. When the secular power passed to Moscow, the churchmen welcomed in their own interest a strong centralizing authority which acknowledged their preeminence in spiritual affairs. As the priesthood added to its worldly power, it reinforced its hold on the instruments of indoctrination. All authority was divine, proclaimed the patriarchs, and the rule of the Muscovite tsars was therefore godlike. This solidarity between the patriarchs and the boyars was crucial to the rise of Muscovy. Through a complex system of marriages, the elite families formed a durable alliance, which was reinforced by a widespread acceptance that unity benefited all members of the elite. The alliances were focused on the supremacy of the tsars, and the church leaders in their turn supported solidarity around the single ruler. From this convergence of secular and spiritual authority arose a unified system of government, able to mobilize the material endowment of the region for renewed economic progress. With such powerful structures of leadership and control, the potential of a difficult terrain could be exploited.

In applying this system, the tsars made use of the lessons they had been taught by their Mongol masters, who opened the way for conversion of the peasantry into a service-bound class. The lessons included ruthless and arbitrary authority, a limitation of the role of the state to the collection of tribute and the maintenance of order, and minimal concern for the well-being of the people. A crude apparatus of control was reinforced by an atmosphere of fear, endorsed by a compliant church. Indeed, the church took the lead in working out an ideology to justify the system, at the cost of undermining any claim it might have had to intellectual independence. Believing that the best interests of all would be served by a monarchy with no limits to its power, the clergy, as the sole source of spiritual authority, spelt out the beneficent inevitability of submission and unquestioning piety. Survival of a settled society in an environment otherwise suited to a nomadic lifestyle may well have depended on such a system of rule and belief.

In the ten years after the death of the Prophet in 632 the Muslims overran Iraq, Syria, Palestine, Egypt and western Iran. During the rest of the century their ships were sailing the Mediterranean, opening the way into southern France and Spain. A century after the Prophet they occupied oasis towns in central Asia, encountered Chinese armies and penetrated Hindu and Buddhist societies in India. This global extension of a religious and military movement was sustained by economic, political and cultural factors by means of which a new civilization was brought into being. The capture of trade routes and areas of surplus output was crucial. The

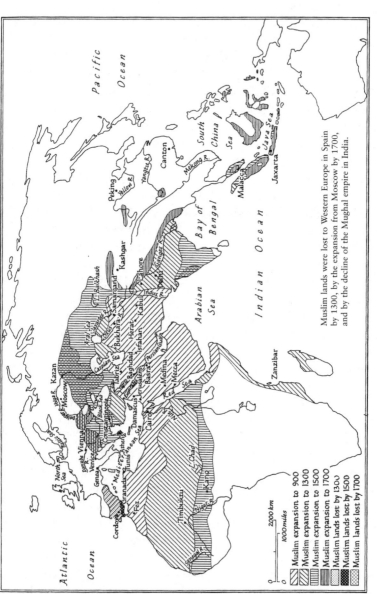

The spread of Islam (to 1700)

Source: I.M. Lapidus, *A History of Islamic Societies*, Cambridge University Press, 1988, p. 243, based on F. Robinson, *Atlas of the Islamic World, 1982* and W.C. Bryce, *An Historical Atlas of Islam*, 1981.

Muslim lands were lost to Western Europe in Spain by 1300, by the expansion from Moscow by 1700, and by the decline of the Mughal empire in India.

Muslim expansion to 900
Muslim expansion to 1300
Muslim expansion to 1500
Muslim expansion to 1700
Muslim lands lost by 1300
Muslim lands lost by 1500
Muslim lands lost by 1700

emergence of urban centres and state institutions provided a network of political control. The ideal of achieving social and economic equality provided the nexus of ideological support.

From the traditions of Persia and Mediterranean civilizations the new Arab rulers in Syria and Iraq adopted a coinage system, a postal service and land and sea communications. The official adoption of the Arabic language facilitated the conversion of regional communities into an overarching identity, and skills such as paper-making and irrigation and the cultivation of different plants spread across the wide domain. With a significant increase in food production there came increases in population and urbanization, and the wealth to sustain a tradition of Muslim science. Nourished by its own philosophical schools and mystical orders such as the Sufis, Islam absorbed medical and mathematical knowledge from various traditions.

Islam made no distinction in theory between church and state: indeed, there was no church as such, but rather a commitment to a body of doctrine deemed to hold sway throughout all activities in the life of a society. The goal, so to speak, was to widen a religion into a civilization. In so doing, Islam had to come to terms first with its own tribal origins and secondly with the cultural maturity of its acquired surroundings. It had also to face some rival interpretations of the faith within its own ranks and to combine overall unity with regional loyalties. In practice, the invading forces of Arabs came as predators: they were in a sense obeying the injunctions of their creed to conquer the infidels and live off their land. After a century of assimilation, Arabs and non-Arabs adopted the norms of an agrarian and trading society. In particular, a client system was brought in from Arabia to secure the cooperation of local people, landowners, village headmen and family patriarchs. Islam found itself aiming at an egalitarian ideal, dedicated to monotheistic principles: on that foundation, there could be unity of faith across an area of wide cultural plurality.

The political state, the army, the treasury, the bureaucracy were in theory to be the instruments of Allah, who was all-powerful and had provided for the needs of all people and would hold them accountable for their deeds on the last day of judgement. All problems were to be resolved by reference to the prophetic revelation, and this included particularly political problems. It was the task of the spiritual leaders to oversee this process and see that society so functioned that believers could perform their religious duties in safety. As the equality of Arab and non-Arab became more accepted, society itself became more functional, resting at its basic level on administrative market towns surrounded by villages. The weakening of the old tribal society and its replacement by the new communal structures allowed the agricultural revolution to spread widely and take a firm hold.

In the second half of the eleventh century, the entry of the Seljuk Turks into western Asia gave the caliphate a further lease of life. Converts to Islam, they ruled in the name of the Abbasids until the destruction of Baghdad by the Mongols in the thirteenth century. The Seljuks provided in their limited kingdoms a stable international order, maintained the trade routes and enabled a civilization based on common beliefs, laws and language to remain in existence. Scholars travelled throughout Islam, promulgating the basic teachings as defined in accepted collections of the prophetic traditions. This network of learning, following much the same paths as the commercial network, survived the Mongol and other irruptions. It was still possible in the fourteenth century to move freely in the 'abode of Islam', the wide-ranging community which was based on the shared sources of Islamic life and experience.

The Muslim statesman, judge and historian Ibn Khaldun was an outstanding example of the movement of scholars and of the threat to Islam from nomadic peoples. Born in Tunis in 1332 he went freely between north Africa and Spain, serving as secretary to the Sultan of Morocco before undertaking diplomatic missions between Granada and Seville. He was personally a victim of the instability of the times, being stripped and robbed on one occasion and on another imprisoned for political intrigue. Seeking solitude from an exhausting life he found refuge in the castle of an Algerian tribe and embarked on an interpretation of history. He described the life cycle of empires, from nomadism through conquest and corruption. His central concept was that social cohesion, enhanced by religious ideology, arose spontaneously in tribes. It carried ruling groups to power until weakened by a combination of political, economic and psychological factors. In his analysis civilization presupposed urbanism, and city life bred degeneracy, while new waves of barbarians continued to arrive in search of an improved existence.

The agricultural revolution which was to transform Chinese society began in the eighth century, and it was then that the government officials and the scholarly class moved closer together. An imperial decree required that a Confucian temple be set up in all the provinces and by this act the sage became in effect the patron saint of government. Colleges were fostered in which studies were concentrated on the classics, and the temples were used to commemorate the achievements of outstanding scholars. The Sung emperors turned away from militarism to develop a more pragmatic civil service, bringing in more able practical scholars by a system of sponsorship which favoured outstanding performance and personal responsibility. Many of the newcomers had no previous experience of administration and were ready to look at new ideas. In the eleventh century, a reforming emperor gave sweeping powers to his chief adviser, Wang-An-shih, who accepted the Confucianist ideal that economic prosperity favoured moral well-being, but went contrary to tradition in proclaiming assertive government roles.

In the twelfth century, criticisms of the failure of the administration were made most outspokenly by the leading Confucianist scholar, Chu Hsi. He petitioned the emperor to practise the traditional virtues himself, to impeach inefficient officials, and not to make a humiliating peace with invading forces in the north. In a turbulent career which included the promotion of agriculture, the patriot scholar called for the

Confucianist principles to be followed again. The original
nature of the state had been good, he declared, but it was no
longer allowed to operate in that way. Instead of the harmonious golden mean, the administration of the country had
moved into a world of selfish desires. Although the views
of Chu Hsi were often too radical for rulers to accept, they
left a lasting impression on Chinese society. The Mongol
occupation occurred at a time when the country was in
full economic expansion. The monetary system continued
to spread and trade was extended into central Asia and
the Middle East. But this was in essence an exploitative
rule which created resentment, directed particularly at foreigners, corrupt officials and a growing gulf between rich and
poor.

The Mongol unification of much of the central Eurasian
land mass had several positive effects, reducing the number
of competing tribute gatherers, assuring greater safety in
travel, and putting China and Europe in direct contact. A
few of the cities at the crossroads of routes grew in size,
particularly if they occupied fertile land or served as religious centres. Samarkand was outstanding among them. The
very success of communications eventually had its sinister
side, however, when a pandemic erupted across the entire
region, causing enormous loss of life and holding up the
development of a potential world system for nearly two
centuries.

When the caravan trade across Eurasia was extended
northwards, wild rodents of the steppe became carriers of
new diseases, among them it is thought the bubonic plague.
From focuses of infection in the region of Manchuria, or
perhaps Burma, the plague appears to have invaded China in
the mid-fourteenth century. Travelling the caravan routes of
Asia to reach the Crimea, and thence Europe and the Near
East, it would have radiated inland from the sea ports,
carried by black rats whose fleas transmitted infection to city
populations. When the climate worsened and caused crop
failures, the densely inhabited areas faced the full force of
what became known as the Black Death. Tending to recur in

later centuries, it affected both economic progress and confidence in rational theology. When recovery returned to the civilized centres of Europe, China and the Middle East, the prevailing ideologies had acquired a more secular edge.

New beginnings

After centuries of political breakdown and economic decline, accompanied by widespread crises of belief, massive movements of population led to a renewal of settlement across the regional zones. New centres of civilization took shape in western Europe, southern China, the Middle East and Russia, stimulating a renewal of economic activity within the zones and to some extent between them. Renewal and advances in agricultural techniques provided the essential surpluses for prosperous and expanding societies and, in a development of craft skills, manufacturing was resumed in old and new materials. The Chinese and the western Europeans in particular made progress in industrial techniques and products, entering into trade across the regions in which the Arabs were effective intermediaries.

Once again the economic needs were paramount, supported by alliances between secular rulers and spiritual leadership. The political systems diverged, reflecting the traditions and the terrain of the different regions, but overall the common pattern was that received religious authority (Christian, Confucian, Muslim) was allied alongside political authority in support of the basic economic drive. The towns flourished as centres of trade and manufacturing, acquiring independent authority and growing strategic roles. Mongol intrusion left permanent marks on Chinese, Russian and Islamic societies, promoting to some extent the intercourse between them but also leading to the movement of plague, which held back the potential of a world trading system.

PART V
Wider Identities

By 1500, the four early modern civilizations were well enough established to envisage wider identities: Islamic empires in the east and the west, Chinese expeditions into southern seas and across northern frontiers, Russian probes into Siberia, and western European oceanic ventures. Left unmolested in the period of Mongol expansion, and developing superior technologies, the Europeans responded longer and more successfully to the global impulse, matching improvements in ships and seafaring with advances in weaponry. In competitive and sometimes hostile encounters, the new nation-states in turn took the lead, until British maritime power, combined with an industrial revolution, opened the way to a different kind of world system. In all these endeavours, the expanding civilizations accompanied their material objectives with missionary commitment to their different belief systems, at first in religious terms, increasingly with secular and political goals. In these powerful movements from the early modern centres of civilization, to enlarge the fields of their influence and activity, the three imperatives – political, economic and ideological – were all at work.

13

Centuries of Empire

Global Impulse Renewed

The period around 1500 is usually presented as the eve of
European expansion and subsequent world domination. This
it certainly was: but it was also a period of expansion by
the contemporary civilizations of China, Islam and Russia.
There were prophets in Peking, Istanbul and Moscow, as well
as in Rome, who saw expanding opportunities and beckon-
ing destinies: and in all these places the prophets were partly
right. Under the Manchu emperors, China did become the
most extensive state in the world. Islamic society did go on
to create vast empires, and none greater than that of the
Ottomans. Russia did adopt a messianic mission, which it
did not relinquish even when the ideology changed. And the
western Europeans did eventually, to a large extent, divide
the globe between them.

The motivation was no longer primarily a search for basic
subsistence, but was rather part of a drive for political identity and independence. Islamic civilization, starting from a
more fertile area with existing trade networks and spurred
by religious zeal, became expansive early on. For a time, such
tendencies were checked by crusades from western Europe
and the undermining of Mongol intrusion, and it was not
until after 1500 that the imperial goals as such became
clear and uncompromising. Modern Chinese civilization, too,
became expansive after the end of the Mongol period: drawn
first into exploring its southern seas and later into securing
its northern frontiers. Russian society responded to Mongol

withdrawal with a prolonged movement to incorporate all the Slavs and to gain access to the open seas. The western Europeans, checked by Islam in the Mediterranean, sought outlets round the African land mass and across the ocean to the west. They had escaped Mongol occupation, but the wars between them persisted into their overseas ventures, in which, by means of superior technology, they were eventually able to outlast the rest. In the rivalries of the nation-states lay the key to their unique success in creating what became a world system.

In expanding their frontiers, the early modern imperialists were fortified also by the conviction that their particular styles of civilization were the best suited to the peoples they were incorporating within their spheres of influence. The Chinese of the Ming dynasty wished to confer upon less cultivated societies all the benefits of their customs and traditions and the special merits of the Confucianist proprieties. The Ottomans took very seriously their injunction to wage holy war, while extending protection to those who accepted Islam and tolerance to other 'peoples of the book'. Both the Russians and the western Europeans were persuaded that there was no greater service they could render than to bring the light of Christian civilization to those who lived in spiritual darkness.

The restoration of a native Chinese dynasty by the Ming after the Mongol interlude was based on the southern part of the country. By 1387 the whole of traditional China had been reunited and an extensive policy was immediately proclaimed: by a great victory in Mongolia in 1388, adhesion of Korea in 1392, and expeditions into central and south-eastern Asia; and it was continued until the middle of the fifteenth century. The main purpose was to establish the prestige of the state throughout the region, and it was the big maritime expeditions which gave it particular significance. A vast programme of reforestation was launched, with the object of constructing a fleet of ships for the high seas. Between 1405 and 1424, seven maritime expeditions were undertaken, each comprising several dozen large junks and carrying over 20,000 men. Landings were made in Sumatra and Java, on the west coast of India, in the Persian Gulf and in east Africa. These voyages, which were accomplished decades before the Portuguese rounded the tip of Africa, were undertaken in a spirit entirely different from that of the western Europeans. A prominent motive was the desire of a confident regime to make itself and its achievements widely known. There was also some desire for trade, partly in prestigious goods, and a genuine interest in securing more accurate information about the outside world. Internal financial crisis and the Mongol menace in the north were among the reasons for ending the expeditions and for the subsequent withdrawal of the Chinese from maritime expansion, although some had settled along the trading routes and China's sphere of influence in Asia remained.

The Ming rulers were succeeded by the Manchu, a border people from the north-east who were partly sinicized and had a highly developed military system. In 1644 they took Peking and by 1681 the whole country had been overrun and consolidation begun. Thus assured, the Manchu gave the Chinese their most expansive phase of development of modern times. Their destiny was to the north, on the steppes where they had won their first victories. Expansion into Mongolia, Tibet and central Asia was undertaken primarily to safeguard the frontiers against the perennial threat of barbarian invasion and to establish stable relations with the steppe peoples. In a great career of conquest, the Manchu forces reached a frontier with Russian civilization. At its widest extent in the mid-eighteenth century their empire covered more than 11 million square kilometres. Inevitably, the influence of this vast realm was felt over a still wider area, penetrating Korea, the Philippines, Vietnam, Siam and Nepal. Known as the Ch'ing empire from the dynastic name adopted by the Manchu, it incorporated many different peoples.

Japan meanwhile, after a century of civil war, was reunited in the early seventeenth century by powerful new rulers who established the Tokugama Shogunate and closed the country off from the outside world. Agricultural output increased

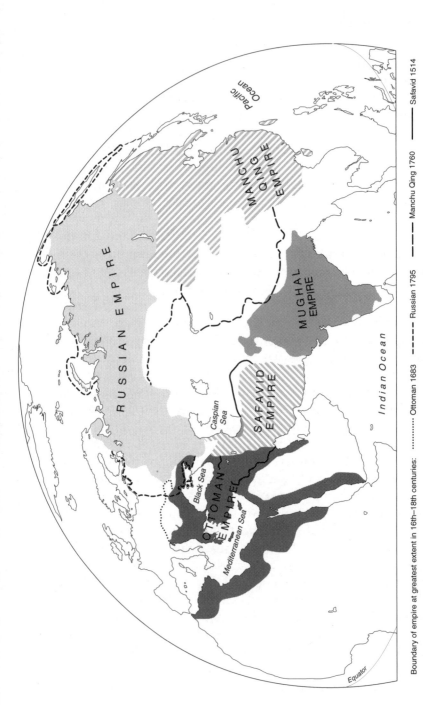

Eurasian land empires (c.1700)

Boundary of empire at greatest extent in 16th–18th centuries: ········· Ottoman 1683 — – — Russian 1795 — - - Manchu Qing 1760 —— Safavid 1514

Source: Based on *Philip's Atlas of World History*, George Philip, 1999, p. 112.

with improved techniques and land reclamation, supported by a return to political and social stability. In a deliberate attempt to move away from Chinese influence, the Shogunate was in effect laying the foundations for a separate civilization, with its own religious antecedents and its own educational and cultural pursuits. Growing population and urbanism were accompanied by the beginnings of industrialization. The scale of growth and change created new political problems, not least in the relationship between the centre in Kyoto and the regional domains.

The sixteenth and seventeenth centuries were for Islam the period of the Mughal empire in the east and the Ottoman empire in the west, with the Safavid dynasty for a time holding the middle lands based on Persia. For Islam had become the religion of virtually all the nomadic Turkish peoples, serving both as a passport to a superior culture and a justification for raids against peoples with other beliefs. Among these were the populations of India, whose cities had acquired considerable wealth. The Turks came first to pillage but remained to rule, merging their ways with the customs of the Hindus while introducing them to Persian culture. By then another group, the Ottoman Turks, had established a new dynasty in Anatolia and were preparing to expand from there. The Safavids were of Iranian stock, but they converted Turkish tribes who were to provide the elite of their fighting forces. Although the regional empires went some distance towards creating separate cultures, the many and diverse societies which were now a part of Islamic civilization still shared a common culture based on religious beliefs.

Expansion into the Indian subcontinent began effectively with the Delhi sultanate, which reached its greatest extent in the first half of the fourteenth century. The Mughal monarchs in the sixteenth century were to have more lasting control, but were less wholly committed to Islam. Akbar's empire encompassed the greater part of the subcontinent. He set himself the task of unifying at least the northern half, introducing Persian as the only official language and attempting to fuse the religion and culture of Islam with the Hindu heritage of most of his subjects. Local rulers were allowed considerable autonomy, subject to the oversight by a centralized military bureaucracy of a mixed ethnic base. Such far-reaching reforms failed to survive his long reign, and Islamic orthodoxy was restored at the end of the seventeenth century by Aurangzeb, with the aim of converting India into a purely Muslim country.

In the Middle East the more successful of the border raiders at the beginning of the fourteenth century had been the Ottomans, and their base in Anatolia soon filled up with wave upon wave of Turkish families looking for a homeland. The Ottomans were fired by the zeal of warriors, reinforced by the high opinion in which they were held for their victories over the Christian states. The culture of the marches came in fact to be dominated by the Islamic concept of the holy war. Like other frontier societies, this was a community of many parts, ethnically and socially, and it tended to obey its own tribal laws. The Ottoman domain was at one and the same time a political institution, a commercial organization and the means of disseminating an ideology.

The idea of a universal empire originated in the later fifteenth century with Mehmed II, who believed 'there should be only one empire, one faith, and one sovereign in the whole world.' He claimed to be the master of two seas and two continents, and his rule remained unshaken for four centuries. Wresting power from Venice, the strongest naval power in the Mediterranean, the Ottoman state fought its way into European politics and would henceforth be a factor in the balance of power there. Another conquering sultan, Selim I, declared his intention to emulate Alexander the Great and turned his attention to the traditional strongholds of Islam in Persia and Egypt. At his death in 1520, Selim had doubled the size of the empire; it stretched from the Caspian to the Adriatic. The final years of expansion came in the next reign by Selim's son, Suleyman. Inheriting an empire that was beginning to dominate eastern Europe, he pushed it further in all directions, using to good effect an efficient and well-equipped machine.

As the civilization centred on Muscovy sprawled outwards, undefined frontiers and lack of access to the open sea
were a continuing source of weakness. The need to be
constantly on the move, imposed by the poverty of the soil
and an unfavourable climate, left a permanent mark on the
society of the steppes; and a political system which gave the
princes outright ownership of the land and its inhabitants
increased their appetite for more. The expansive phase under
the tsars lasted for three centuries or more, from Ivan the
Great at the end of the fifteenth century to Catherine the
Great at the end of the eighteenth. It had three main aspects:
the conquest of neighbouring territories, the ingathering of
the Slavs, and the penetration of Siberia.

The core of the process was the land around the rival cities
of Moscow and Novgorod. With the conquest of Novgorod
in 1478, Ivan established a claim to its vast principality to
the north and east and began the systematic elimination of
potential rivals there. Early in the next century, he extended
Russian control over large areas to the west and south, followed by Ivan IV, who made significant advances in the
south-east. By the conquest of the khanate of Kazan, he
opened a way across the Urals into Siberia; and, by the conquest of the khanate of Astrakhan, he gained control of the
Volga basin to the Caspian Sea. An influential figure in the
Muscovite expansion was the Metropolitan Macarius who,
as well as urging the tsar to push towards the east and open
a new field of missionary activity, worked out an elaborate
genealogy to prove that the rulers of Moscow were the heirs
of an imperial line back to the emperor Augustus. This fitted
well with the idea of Moscow as the 'third Rome' (formulated by the monk Philotheus of Pskov), which became
an integral part of official Muscovite political theory and
of the proposition that the rulers of Russia were universal
Christian sovereigns.

The heartlands around the upper Volga were now effec-
tively enclosed on all sides by territories reaching towards the
Black Sea and the Baltic. Kazan had opened the way into
Siberia, which, although colonized with astonishing speed,

remained the most thinly occupied area. The official date given for the start of the penetration is 1583, when a group of merchants and manufacturers received from Ivan IV large land concessions beyond the Urals and commissioned an exploratory survey. The main economic resource was the fur-bearing fauna of the great Siberian forests. In pursuit of it the trappers moved, in the course of a century, the entire distance to the Pacific, followed by traders, settlers, scientists and government officials. The settlements along the southern borders of the forests were sparse and cultivation there was poorly rewarded, but until the government claimed the territory the settlers were free of interference.

Expansion was resumed under Alexis in the mid-seventeenth century. At his death Russia was a great power, at least in terms of its extent. But it still lacked access to the open sea, and achieving this in the west became the objective of Peter the Great. At a second attempt, Azov was captured at the mouth of the Don and possession was confirmed by a treaty with the Ottomans. Plans to push on into the Black Sea area were abandoned, however, in the absence of effective allies, and Peter turned north to the Baltic. Early in the eighteenth century, the Swedes were defeated on land and at sea, and the eastern shores of the Baltic were ceded to the Russians. Peter had already constructed the new city of St Petersburg where the Neva flowed into the Gulf of Finland, and he proclaimed it as his capital. The long reign of Catherine the Great completed the major period of tsarist expansion. The Russian empire then extended nominally halfway round the world between frontiers with Germany and China.

Meanwhile the western Europeans had been opening up the seaways and their scientists were sketching improved outlines of the physical universe. Copernicus, the son of a Baltic merchant, became dissatisfied with earth-centred ideas and developed the theory that the earth, with other planets, revolved about a point near the sun. His 'system of the world' was published in the sixteenth century and was systematized in the next century by the Dutch mathematician Johann

Kepler in terms of a dynamic equilibrium of mechanical forces. Exploring uncharted seas, European sailors were to be helped increasingly by a scientific charting of the heavens. As exploration progressed, world charts improved in range and accuracy. The most celebrated of a new generation of cartographers was the Portuguese Ribiero, whose sixteenth-century marine chart was a major landmark in the development of knowledge of the world.

Portugal was the earliest of the Atlantic nations to break the oceanic barrier. Profitable settlements were established in the Madeiras and the Azores, and this encouraged further exploration. Expeditions to the west African coast opened up trade in pepper and ivory, gold and slaves. The Portuguese were also the first round the African land mass and, from the coasts of east Africa, they ventured to India and Siam and even China, supporting their trading activities with well-placed forts. The main penetration of the western hemisphere was by the Spanish, who found precious metals and unlimited grazing for their cattle. In Mexico, they looted and destroyed original civilizations, killed many of the inhabitants, intermarried with the survivors and settled to the overlordship of an agrarian society. The Aztec civilization and the Inca civilization were abruptly terminated, a consequence in part of the introduction of contagious diseases in densely settled areas, undermining indigenous belief systems and the will to resist.

In the Indian Ocean the Portuguese were challenged by the Dutch, who became for a time the world's most successful naval and commercial nation, penetrating all the known oceans and warring against all their rivals. Well behind came the French and the English, the former entangled in European affairs and allowing the initiative to pass from them. The north American seaboard colonies were founded at intervals during the first half of the seventeenth century, variously sponsored for royal, religious and commercial purposes. The French ceded ascendancy there and in India, where the collapse of the Mughal empire left a vacuum into which the trading companies and their home governments were drawn.

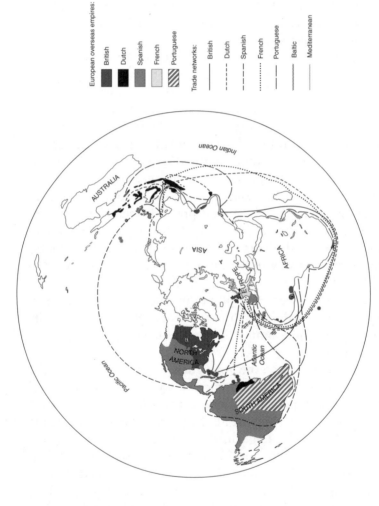

World trading empires (1770)

Source: Based on *Philip's Atlas of World History*, George Philip, 1999, p. 115.

By the end of the eighteenth century, British dominion was established and India became Britain's most important overseas asset, replacing the American colonies, which seceded in 1776.

Somewhat in the manner of the Tokugawa Shogunate in Japan, the American colonists intended a different society from the one they had left behind in Europe. Tackling the economic problem of subsistence, they introduced tobacco plantations into Virginia, exploited existing resources of fish, fur and timber in Massachusetts, and established mixed farming in Pennsylvania, clearing as they went the vast area of forest cover between the Atlantic seaboard and the Mississippi. In support of their growing economies the colonies devised separate political systems and modified their initial religious commitments. The American Revolution embodied the basic elements of the formative period, in a commitment to rising living standards, republicanism and independence, and an ideology of millennial aspirations and a lessening of sectarian differences. The declaration in 1776, in confirming the intention to create a separate and different society, laid the foundations for a new civilization.

In the last quarter of the eighteenth century an industrial breakthrough in Britain transformed the prospects for world trade, and political revolution in France gave currency to libertarian ideas which eventually affected all European overseas possessions. As the new processes of industrialism spread, it was trade rather than territory that became the main goal, providing raw materials for the factories and foodstuffs to meet growing domestic demand.

14

Tools of Empire

Technology of Expansion

The technology of empire building lay crucially in the fields of maritime transport, armaments and communications. There were advances in all these areas in all early modern civilizations by the time they began to enlarge their fields of operation. Together they contributed decisively to a cumulative process which eventually launched an industrial revolution. Progress was uneven, however, both between the regions and between the main kinds of innovation. China was at first in a position of potential leadership, but was left behind by the western Europeans; and printing, although in principle of enormous importance, lagged behind shipbuilding and weaponry. The origin of these disparities has been seen to lie in the different priorities of ruling elites, which were predominantly military in Europe and predominantly literary in China. Eventually, as the European thrust prevailed, the stimulus given to general industrial advance set in train changes of revolutionary significance. In this chapter, attention is given to shipbuilding and seafaring, to the role of gunpowder and canonry, and finally to greater knowledge and skills across metallurgy and mechanization in the course of the nineteenth century.

Maritime activity had a long tradition in the China seas, and large vessels of several decks were being built before the end of the T'ang period. In the eleventh century, warships were built capable of carrying horses below decks and soldiers above, and there is evidence of naval manoeuvres on the Yangtse in the late twelfth century. Reputedly one of the most efficient vessels under sail ever constructed, the Chinese junks were then the largest, strongest and most seaworthy ships in the world. In their rigging they were far ahead of western patterns, and they had the benefit of massive rudders and controlled steering. They varied in size, the largest being at least ten times the tonnage of the ships used by Columbus, and some were equipped with cannon.

Mediterranean shipbuilding, both Arab and European, was in advance of that in the northern seas, responding to the earlier quickening of commercial activity. As early as the twelfth century, some Genoese ships had two decks, and three-deckers appeared in the thirteenth. At the time of the Ming voyages, the forces of Islam were penetrating the Indian ocean, using the triangular sails known as lateens which were more easily manoeuvred than square rigs. When this design reached the Atlantic coasts, it was to encounter different constructions. Progress there had been somewhat slow after the Viking innovations, and the ships that carried the Norman invasion army to England were hardly distinguishable from the vessels of two centuries before. The northern merchantman was developed in about the fourteenth century into the cog, which remained the standard design for some centuries. Among the improvements were the fighting towers known as castles and the large spars, known as bowsprits, to give greater effect to the sails. A combination of the lateen with the square rig enabled mariners to face conditions in most waters. The stern rudder had been adopted some time earlier than it was in the Mediterranean, and the addition of the magnetic compass and the astrolabe fitted ships to venture further, leading in turn to a sharp increase in the size of cargo vessels.

The Ottoman Turks, who were in their origins horsemen rather than seamen, were obliged to take to the waters to assert their supremacy against the European powers. For this purpose, they adopted the centuries-old craft of the region, the galley propelled primarily by teams of oarsmen. The galley fleets of the Ottomans were able to defeat the Venetians, who until then had been the paramount sea power in the Mediterranean. The Turks had commissioned an unprecedented programme of shipbuilding, followed by a considerable development of commercial activity. Later in the sixteenth century, Suleyman reinforced their naval claims when a great shipyard at Istanbul equipped him with a powerful fleet. A plan to keep the Muscovites out of the lower Volga and put a Turkish fleet in the Caspian was a failure, but a new fleet was promptly fitted out with an improved armament and another was sent into the Red Sea to challenge the Portuguese.

Although the early voyages of discovery were not made by fighting ships, naval armament soon became important and it remained so until modern times. In this respect, the Europeans gained and sustained a clear superiority. By the fifteenth century an essential contribution to this result was made by the combination of cannon and chemistry. In weaponry as in shipbuilding, the Muslim states were exploitative rather than innovative, using for example what they learned from Byzantium about firepots and projectile engines, without improving either the pyrotechnical or ballistic techniques. The knowledge of gunpowder, originating in China, probably reached Europe through Islam and was first used in the fourteenth century. At about the same time, cannon began to be cast from cupreous metal and, by the fifteenth century, a new technical literature of chemistry and metallurgy was circulating in manuscript. The Venetians may have been the first to use ship-borne artillery and by the middle of the century the practice was common. By the sixteenth century, the number of guns on board was such as to prompt a revolution in the design of ships and the tactics of naval warfare.

The largest industrial undertaking in western Europe was the arsenal in Venice. After the Ottoman successes, the city's ruling council declared in 1521 that 'one of the chief factors in the protection of lands and armies is the artillery.' By about 1500, there were pistols, hand grenades, bayonets and shells in use by the European powers. The total demand for munitions, for sea and land use, led to a steady increase in mining and played a part in preparing for increased industrial activity. Metallurgical operations in particular benefited from the need for more powerful guns to be cast without adding overmuch to their weight, and improved forced-draught furnaces produced purer metal while using less fuel.

The Portuguese were the first to use armed strength in eastern waters, not only to outgun the Muslim traders but also to force trade from reluctant Indians and engage in outright aggression. The spice trade was of particular importance to the Arabs and, to wrest it from them, the Portuguese had first to defeat them in open conflict and then establish land bases. In the encounters on the open sea and in the ensuing control of the Malabar coast, gunnery was the decisive factor. The Asian potentates hastened to arm their ships, which were however ill-designed for the purpose. The Portuguese remained unbeatable in eastern seas until the Dutch and the English arrived with better ships and better guns. The Atlantic carrying trade pioneered by the Spaniards in the sixteenth century stimulated a growth in the size of ships and in the arming of galleons to protect their convoys and their cargoes of precious metals.

In the siege of Constantinople by the Ottoman Turks in 1453, gunpowder missiles known as bombards battered down walls that had withstood years of attack. Traditional fortifications were indeed coming under attack everywhere. The power structure of all the Muslim imperial states was military, and gunpowder weaponry gave them a new asset in overcoming local resistance. Against this force, the strength of isolated strongholds declined, destructive nomadism was checked, cities were brought under closer bureaucratic control and local governors were obliged to give way to organized power centres. Superior armament gave the Ottomans a clear advantage over the Safavids in the Persian campaigns, when a formidable combination of musketry and mortar power proved an insuperable barrier to cavalry. The most outstanding Safavid ruler, Shah Abbas I, did resort belatedly to arms technology, casting cannon and instructing new fighting units in their use. In India, meanwhile, the Mughals had not been inattentive to the technology of armaments and shipbuilding. Aurangzeb in particular seems to have been well equipped with artillery. His country was capable at that time of producing crucible-fired steel of good quality, perhaps even ahead of the Europeans. There were serviceable naval shipyards near Bombay, and there were workshops which produced anchors, guns and cannon, as well as fine sidearms, swords and daggers, and even rifles.

The intimate relationship between military and naval strength and national economic resources had become increasingly apparent during the almost endless campaigns for western European dominance. The cost brought more than one of the competing nations to the edge of bankruptcy as they sought to pay for swelling armies and large-scale naval encounters; and the efficient market economies of the Dutch and the English gave them the advantage over the Spanish and the French. The wealth to be derived from overseas ventures was both a means of filling war chests and a reason for extending the wars from Europe to the oceans and beyond. From the mid-seventeenth century, national interests replaced religious divisions as the main cause of wars, and the ships and armaments needed to conduct them stimulated the growth of the industries that supplied them.

From that time, the imperialist rivalries of the European nation-states were concentrated on competition for export markets and overseas supplies. In the late eighteenth century, a series of inventions in the textile and iron industries gave Britain an early lead. Many factors were involved, ranging from a prior spurt in agricultural productivity and resulting population growth, through the availability of internal transport on rivers and canals, and of capital and credit for investment, to increased demand both at home and overseas. British entrepreneurs, who have been credited with a favourable attitude of mind at that time towards the possibility of profit, monopolized overseas trade sufficiently to make an industrial revolution not only practicable but also a condition of further progress.

Improved technical devices in the woollen industry, spreading crucially to cottons, accelerated a move to production in factories. This in turn stimulated changes in the metallurgical industry to provide the machines, and to the introduction of the steam engine to drive them. The mechanization of metallurgy and transport and the increasing power of engines and boilers demanded increasing supplies of more accurate metal parts. This led to machine tools capable of making parts for other machines; and in the outstanding period of industrial progress, machines combining several functions could be moved by a single transmission system. Increasing precision in mechanical engineering marked the 1830s and 1840s, heralding a powerful expansion of the metallurgical industries, using blast furnaces powered by steam.

The resulting increase in the productivity of labour was substantial and continuous. By 1830, Britain was producing half of Europe's cotton goods and iron, three-quarters of Europe's mined coal, and most of Europe's steam engines. As the stimulus spread to the means of transportation, massive investment began in the world's first railway system, of which 5,000 miles were put into operation between 1840 and 1850. The pre-eminence of Britain at mid-century was undisputed. With 2 per cent of the world's population and only 10 per cent of Europe's, the United Kingdom had a capacity in modern industry equal to 40–45 per cent of the world potential. In parallel was an international system of finance based on London; and the English language was used in all continents. Canals were cut to break land barriers, such as the Suez Canal in 1869, and by 1883 one firm had laid 13,000 miles of submarine cables, enough to go halfway round the world. Linked with land wires, for example to India through the Middle East, they enabled messages to be telegraphed at speed over long distances.

By this time, the expansion of printing was experiencing a long delayed technological transformation. After the independent invention in Europe of metallic movable type around 1450, there had been little technical development for three centuries, although books on industrial processes undoubtedly helped the development of new skills, particularly in metallurgy. The first significant step came in 1814, with the harnessing of steam power to a reciprocating type-bed to turn out printed sheets four times faster than the output of hand presses. This was followed by the conversion to rotary action, which made printing continuous, and by the 1860s a completely automatic press had become possible using long rolls of paper. By the 1880s, typecasting and typesetting had been mechanized by the invention of the Linotype machine.

In the latter part of the nineteenth century a large expansion also began in the chemical industry, which had important outlets in the manufacture of armaments. Improvements in guns and in the quality of gunpowder were being made in nearly all countries, calling for high tensile steels, the invention of shrapnel, and new types of explosive including dynamite. The machine gun came into use by the end of the century, with the development of a smokeless powder. With the coming of the dynamo and power stations, electricity was in use for lighting, traction and industry in Europe, America and Japan.

By the 1870s rapid industrial revolutions had spread to Belgium, France, Germany and the United States. The British lead was reduced in particular by the Germans and the Americans; and by the 1880s Russian and Japanese economic developments had increased their impact on international diplomacy and the balance of power. Railway construction played a major role in America and Russia, contributing to the emergence of global trends. An acceleration in the rate of change after 1865 transformed the United States into the leading industrial superpower, and by 1900 both America and Japan were embarking on expansionist policies.

15

Creeds of Empire

Ideologies on the Move

The early attitudes of the Chinese and Muslim empire builders were largely inspired by an intention to spread the teachings of Confucius and Muhammad. The empire builders of Russia and western Europe were partly inspired by a desire to promote Christianity, but that intention was mixed from the outset with more material motives, which were freely acknowledged. The superior technology of the Europeans eventually gave greater weight to their ideology and shifted the emphasis towards economic exploitation and military dominance. The commitment to Christian missionary activity shifted towards a social gospel of welfare and economic betterment. Finally, the ideologies which had arisen out of the political and industrial revolutions became influential on a global scale, challenging the traditional beliefs of the other civilizations while instilling revolutionary ferment throughout western Europe and Russia.

After the Mongol withdrawal, the Chinese under the Ming needed to bring about peaceful conditions in what was the world's largest state. 'Those who have surrendered', it was decreed, 'should be moved within the empire so that they may submit to the teachings of our sages, gradually learn our rites and etiquette and change their old customs.' A flood of regulations and admonitions was sent out to encourage diversified peoples to conform to an ideal society. In the north, the Mongols who had stayed behind accepted this doctrine. In the south, the aboriginal peoples were allowed some freedom to be governed in their traditional ways, but Chinese suzerainty involved acquiring some cursory knowledge of the Confucian proprieties.

The investiture of local rulers by the Ming emperors was intended to impress them with the majesty of the court and the glory of the empire. Provincial officials, as well as super-vising law and order, were required to disseminate conven-tional morality. In extending their reach by overland missions and maritime expeditions, the Ming sought, by cultural ap-peal as much as by military power, to announce that a new post-Mongol period existed. By the seventeenth century, this motivation had waned as Confucianist officials discouraged further foreign penetration and factions led to divided coun-sels and imperial inaction. It was left to the Manchu rulers to resume the practice of ideological dissemination.

The Manchu faced a long-term task of adapting to Chinese culture and institutions, but they took the challenge very seri-ously. Their suspicion of the motives of Christian missionar-ies led in 1670 to the issue of a sacred edict which stressed the Confucianist virtues of filial piety, encouraged the ven-eration of scholarship and urged a disregard of false doc-trines. By mastering Chinese methods and outlook, they became legitimate contenders for the rule of what they saw as the centre of the civilized world. By their conquests in central Asia, they indeed became the rulers of the biggest and probably the richest state of the eighteenth century. In so doing, they willingly accepted as one of their most essential tasks the inauguration of Confucian orthodoxy throughout vast domains and in all strata of society. In thus stressing and enforcing the inherited ideology, the Manchu rulers were acting from the most obvious of political motives. They had a fundamentally authoritarian conception of imperial rule, requiring from all their subjects respectful submission and unfailing loyalty; and this was reinforced by the Confucian-ist orthodoxy which proclaimed the virtues of obedience.

The spread of Islamic doctrines in the empires of the Ottomans and the Mughals was impeded by the entrenched position of other powerful religions, Christianity in Europe and Hinduism in India. The political attraction of the new dominant regimes had some effect, but it was most crucially the holy men who were able to adapt their teachings to prevailing beliefs and practices. In the result, Islam in the empires was both an international creed based on learning and law and also a locally modified fusion of customs and commitments. To secure adhesion to their regimes, the political rulers tended to absorb the leading scholars into the bureaucracies and patronize the Sufis. Intellectual discussion was in the process often suppressed and the quality of religious leadership declined. Despite a not inconsiderable conversion to Islam, the majority of the subject populations remained loyal to their traditional beliefs.

The Ottoman empire had begun as a holy war at the expense of the Christian powers and its prevailing ideology was the creed of the Prophet in its mainstream Sunni version. The sultan required his grand vizier and provincial governors to see that it guided the administration of justice. The officials in the mosques, the teachers in the schools, the lawyers in the courts, all operated within a single system which controlled public opinion. Provided they were loyal and obedient, the various communities – whether religious, functional or regional – were able to live in accordance with their own beliefs and customs. As the empire expanded and provinces were added piecemeal, these concerns continued to apply. Control was strictest where the vital commercial life of the empire was involved, in the great cities and their plains, and on the coast and in the river valleys. In the more remote mountainous areas, provided taxes were paid and there were no encroachments on the central power, local practices were tolerated. It was a religious duty of the state, taken seriously by its agents, to see to the prosperity of all its subjects, and the pious foundations offered a range of public services.

In India, the Delhi sultanate recognized the suzerainty of the caliphs in Baghdad and accepted a duty to defend Islam and its territories. Under their rule the Sufi orders undertook missionary work, helping to build up Muslim communities which included native converts alongside the descendants of immigrants. The Mughal sultans were more ideologically motivated. Akbar's aim in the sixteenth century was to raise himself from the leadership of the minority group to become the accepted ruler of a political empire. With this aim, he revived the idea of divine kingship familiar both in India and in Persia, hoping to secure the devotion of both Muslims and Hindus. He had in mind a universalist creed to which followers of all religions might subscribe, but a militant orthodox role was later restored at the expense of the Hindu religion. The increasing influence of British administration introduced a third stream of ideas, to which the Indian mind reacted with a political movement against foreigners and a transformation of traditional society, leading to the growth of nationalism.

In one respect at least, the doctrines carried by Muscovites into a wider frame resembled those of the Muslim imperialists: they were at two different levels, one closely allied with the political ruling class, the other preached by non-attached holy men. In both civilizations, church and state had been closely aligned, and in Russia the link was strengthened by the claim that Moscow represented the convergence of all the Christian realms. In the seventeenth century, a re-examination of this mission by the Orthodox Church precipitated the 'great schism', which left a reformed church hierarchy attached to the official bureaucracy, while dissenting 'old believers' took to the frontiers to teach more personal forms of their religion. While the reformers, under the patriarch Nikon, aimed at a predominant position throughout the whole orthodox world, the dissenters sought refuge in small communities, where they proved admirably sturdy colonizers. While the official church lost its religious commitment in pursuing political goals in the Slav lands to the west, the sectarians identified with the new settlements in the east in a revival of zeal.

Russian penetration across the Urals, which began in the sixteenth century, was given the character of a holy mission, although in practice its motivation was basically materialist, inspired by the prospect of profit as well as the spirit of adventure and the desire for a freer life. With help from the dissenters, the pioneers organized themselves into disciplined self-governing communities, exploiting the wealth of the forests and claiming tribute from the Tatar khanate. The theme of a Christian mission to the heathen, coupled with an intention to oppose Muslim influence in the area, continued into the eighteenth century, coupled with official satisfaction that the incorporation of Siberia had doubled the size of the empire. The positive benefits of Christian civilization were still being affirmed in the nineteenth century, with the added argument that the teaching of agriculture to nomadic peoples was bound to be of advantage to them. By this time, doctrines of Slavism and Russification were assuming prominence in the west.

In the early nineteenth century, a debate arose over claims to moral superiority over all the peoples of Europe. Both sides, whether 'slavophils' or 'westerners', accepted that Russia had a mission in the field of social policy. Their differences centred on religion, the slavophils being devout Christians and their opponents atheistically inclined. The slavophils also idealized a largely imaginary past, when there was supposed to have been harmony between the people and an autocratic leader. Their ideas later gave way to panslavism, a doctrine closely identified with the expansionist aims of the Russian state. There were some small Slav nations outside the Russian empire, and it was argued that it would be natural for them to accept the Russians as leaders. It was against this background that Russification became official policy. Over half the population of the empire was non-Russian, separated from the 'great Russians' by geography, language and sometimes religion. From the new Baltic provinces to the steppes of Siberia, the pattern of government had at first been to allow some local autonomy, but increasingly this policy was modified in the interests of a system calling for a common loyalty. A new generation of bureaucrats, averse to regional variety and avid for uniformity, were the main authors of the latest imperial ideology.

The western Europeans admitted from the beginning that there were some mercenary as well as missionary motives for their endeavours. Vasco da Gama told the Indians frankly that the Portuguese had come in search of both Christians and spices; and the Spaniard Diaz wrote that he and the other conquistadores in the Indies aimed to serve their god and their king, 'to give light to those who were in darkness, and to grow rich'. Religious zeal was undoubtedly present in an intention to convert unbelievers, if necessary by force, but there was also an intention to safeguard the colonies of settlers by defending Christians and eliminating their adversaries. The Spanish and Portuguese monarchs tended to regard their overseas possessions as papal grants of land in return for an obligation to spread the Christian gospel. At one time every expedition was required to carry missionaries, and the religious orders were particularly active in the mission fields, notably the Jesuits, who gained a remarkable ascendancy over the Indian mind.

In Asia, the missionaries encountered other civilizations with their own systems of belief and their own learned classes. In south-east Asia newly established dynasties had revitalized Theravada Buddhism and Confucianism, and Burma, Siam and Vietnam were subject to state-sponsored forms of religion and culture. In India, China and Japan, the Jesuits tried to make Christianity acceptable by accommodating local customs, such as the caste system and reverence for ancestors. This led to doubts whether basic Christian doctrines were being compromised, and eventually the Jesuits were withdrawn. The Protestant missionaries were generally given feebler support than the Catholics, and the net result of Christian endeavour in the east prior to 1700 was neither very deep nor enduring. What did impress other societies with which the western Europeans came into contact was the division within their own ranks, both political and religious, and above all their commitment to economic enrichment.

Eventually the emphasis of missionary ideology shifted from the benefits of Christian belief to those of a technical and industrial society and, with these benefits, came newer political ideologies. Eighteenth-century Europeans had not doubted that their civilization represented the peak of human achievement, and their nineteenth-century successors had the technology and above all the firepower to prove it. Other societies seemed to them to be locked into immobility, failing to apply the latest discoveries and adhering to customs that were at best pathetic and at worst malign. Missionary Christian zeal certainly did not diminish, and western European arts of healing and administration did undoubtedly bring some real benefits to societies overseas. As the major mission fields expanded, in Africa, India and the Far East, Europeans became the bearers of a social gospel of economic progress, the assumptions of an advanced industrial society. When the Europeans first set about creating their trading and plantation empires overseas, they had used the doctrine of natural law to provide a rationale for forcing other societies into commercial intercourse. When, in the nineteenth century, the British led the way in creating an international system favourable to their own industrial pre-eminence, they used the argument that a division of labour would benefit everyone in a richer and more harmonious world.

Since 1815 the United States had responded to geographical expansion with an economic transformation which replaced an agrarian society with a rapidly growing system of capitalism. While the settlement of the west followed the agrarian pattern, a new scale of cotton production took over in the south, and an industrial revolution in the north proved decisive in the Civil War. The railroads played a decisive role in the settlement of the west and in creating a national market. The extent and pace of economic growth before, during and after the Civil War offered rewards for enterprise which focused attention on material success. The phrase 'Manifest Destiny' came to summarize the expansionist ambitions of a nation behind the conviction that America was both the land of opportunity and one in which a morally improving life could be lived.

In Japan the Tokugawa regime extended its control from Kyoto to the provinces by a system of land and sea routes. Used for the transport of goods throughout the archipelago, these routes facilitated population mobility and led to substantial increases in urbanization. The replacement of the regime in 1867 opened Japan to outside influences. A code of loyalty to the emperor was introduced, according him divine status as the benevolent patriarch of the nation. Modelling developments on the West, the Japanese introduced modern systems of finance, communications and compulsory education. By 1900 Japan had joined the ranks of imperialist states, adopting their ideologies and behaving like them overseas.

Wider identities

Between 1500 and 1900 the four regional civilizations of western Europe, China, Russia and Islam responded to the impulse to enlarge their fields of operation, and among the sequels were the formation of independent civilizations in north America and the Japanese islands.

The four centuries from 1500 were prominently the centuries of empire in the modern era, but unlike the land empires of the classical era there was a strong maritime element as the Muslims sailed the Mediterranean, the Chinese sailed the southern seas, and the western Europeans opened up the Atlantic route to the east. European advances in ship design were supported by Chinese innovations in steering; and knowledge of gunpowder, also spreading from China, gave the Europeans superiority in naval armament. In clashes with the other civilizations and competition between the nation-states, the Europeans opened Asia and the Americas to trade and conquest in which commercial motives were mixed with Christian missionary endeavour. The Russians and the Chinese extended their political influence and ideas into central Asia, and Muslim empires reached from Asia Minor to India.

In all these areas religious ideals were compromised by encounters with rival creeds and secular ideologies, and eventually by the belief systems of the Europeans as their political and industrial revolutions made an impact worldwide.

PART VI
Global Tendencies

By the end of the nineteenth century, the European world economy had enlarged its frame still further to take in new zones in an emerging world system, in which two more modern civilizations, the American and the Japanese, were beginning to become involved. Differing from earlier empires, which had been of political origin, this new system was based on a capitalist mode of production and trade, in which the local economic interests of the peripheral areas became subservient to the economic demands of the core societies. Viewed in one sense as the formative phase of a potential global civilization, the system in its economic role went on to recruit political and military penetration and control to its support. Between 1850 and 1950 hostile encounters became increasingly global, merging eventually into two world wars and the break-up of the politically based empires. In a postwar resurgence led by the American economy, a network of global transport, electronic communications and multinational finance opened up the possibility of alternative solutions.

16

The World Economy

From Crisis to Growth

It has been a central theme of this work that continuing subsistence is the essential precondition of human societies, and that a surplus over and above subsistence is the essential precondition of societies that create permanent civilized centres. In the eighteenth and into the nineteenth centuries, exchanges between the regions became the main source of the surplus of the western European nation-states, particularly Britain and France, and eventually predominantly Britain. This became possible with the opening of the world's oceans to regular shipping; and the lead was taken by Britain because of its maritime pre-eminence. Other areas were increasingly incorporated in what began to take the form of a world system as economic surpluses were siphoned off for the benefit of the western European core centres. This extended both to areas lying outside the other regional centres and to the other regional centres themselves. In this way, penetration of the Chinese, Islamic and Russian centres of civilization brought changes in their patterns of production and trade which contributed to a larger global total.

The colonization by western Europeans of temperate zones in the north and south hemispheres had an immense and lasting impact on the occupations and lifestyles of the Americas and Australasia. In similar climates the colonists settled fertile parts favourable to wheat and cattle. The population of Australia became for a time almost all European in origin and that of New Zealand about nine-tenths. A route to the inland plains opened Australia to a vast area of sheep rearing in the mid-nineteenth century, and after 1870 the invention of refrigerated shipping stimulated meat exports from New Zealand. The economies of the Latin American republics, which became predominantly European, depended in the nineteenth century on the export of raw materials and, with the development of steamships and railways, of other primary products. From initial settlement on the Atlantic coast the Canadians followed tracks opened up by fur traders to the west, completing the Pacific Railroad by 1885 and adding new provinces by 1912.

By this time modern American and modern Japanese civilizations had moved through a formative period into an enlargement of their fields of operation. Expanding westward by means of annexations, negotiated settlements and financial deals, the United States established its own internal empire from the Atlantic to the Pacific and began to extend overseas. Proclaiming moral superiority, the Americans claimed an increasing role in world affairs, based on industrial growth and corporate overseas expansion. The Japanese, driven by the need for raw materials, looked to the mainland, defeating China and Russia in open conflict and acquiring Formosa and Korea and a foothold in Manchuria. The 'unequal treaties' were revised and an alliance was concluded with Britain.

The final phase of expansion came in the last quarter of the nineteenth century in a scramble for territory in which most of the nation-states engaged. Questions of prestige became important in a climate in which rational considerations were overborne by nationalist fervour, prompted in part by the recent unifications of the German and Italian peoples. Believing it to be a mark of inferiority to lack colonies, they joined in the global grab. Economic imperialism gave way to naked political imperialism in which all the excesses of rival states were revived. In 1875 two-thirds of the land surface of the world was dominated by Europeans and the last great carving up of Africa had still to run its course. By then, the capitalist world economy was clearly prefigured, as also was the threat that western European rivalry would trigger global conflict.

By the end of the nineteenth century the process was intensifying, with a global search for raw materials and the accompanying political rivalries of the nation-states. The difficulties of administering territories so feverishly acquired were straining resources to the limit and at a time when western Europe and its constituent parts were becoming internally divisive. The four civilizations had become unstable, with threats to traditional lifestyles and consequent attempts to reconcile them with more progressive beliefs. By the early twentieth century, American civilization too was investing heavily in the global system of capitalism. When the opportunities for further profitable and sustained investment contracted in the third decade, the stock market plunged into speculation on a scale that the available credit mechanism was unable to sustain. Replacing in some ways the leading commercial role of the British, the American economy failed to exercise an effective control and plunged into a prolonged recession, with effects that were felt worldwide.

Between 1929 and 1932, manufacturing in the world as a whole fell by a third, with still greater decreases in America and Germany. International trade and investment also fell by a third, with exports from industrial countries particularly badly affected. International lending virtually ceased. Thirty million people were known to be unemployed, while huge stocks of goods accumulated unsold. The global economic structure built up over several centuries appeared to have gone into deep decline. In the failure to devise an effective concerted response, governments sought to protect their own economies with measures which served only to make matters worse. By 1937 some recovery was in sight, but it was only when political instability led to rearmament that world production rose to new levels. From 1939, arms production soared in conditions of total mobilization, bequeathing to the postwar period a pent-up demand for consumer goods and new construction.

America emerged from the war with unchallenged economic and military supremacy. In the process of securing raw materials and access to foreign markets for manufactures, the Americans undertook substantial increases in overseas investment, reinforced with grants and loans and military expenditure and by the acquisition of overseas manufacturing capacity. Linking commercial interests with a global campaign against what was perceived as a threat of world communism, America took the lead in a war in Korea which had the indirect effect of reviving the Japanese economy. Between 1952 and 1956, the payments for American troops and bases and procurement orders financed a quarter of Japan's commodity imports. In profiting from this windfall, the output of the Japanese was soon way beyond prewar levels. A new industrial thrust came from high technology in chemicals and engineering. Learning quickly what the Americans had to teach, the Japanese were soon ready to supply their former enemies, assisted by low defence spending, high productive investment and a cheap and plentiful labour supply.

As the economies of the world recovered from the destruction of the wars, a new secular ideology began to capture the hearts and minds of peoples in all societies and influence the policies of their governments. This was the doctrine of economic growth as a basis for ever rising living standards, a materialist substitute for the spiritual goals which were coming to be widely questioned. Between the free enterprise societies and the centrally planned societies, alternative means of securing growth were propounded and put to the test. All the modern civilizations became involved, though in different ways and with different results, and the slow but persistent recognition of this common objective further influenced the moves towards global arrangements. Both intergovernmental initiatives and the pursuit of corporate profit-making drew the civilizations closer together within the developing framework of world markets.

The western Europeans adopted as government policies the maintenance of full employment, rising incomes and price stability. Trade unions, which had given support in Britain to wartime restrictions, were now given a voice alongside industrial managements in the choice of appropriate instruments, which included the nationalization of basic industry and the creation of planning organizations. In tripartite consultation across industry, economic growth was accepted as the national target and as such was a key element in government policy. With variations linked to their national traditions, this was the pattern adopted in Britain, Germany, Italy and the Scandinavian countries. When planning and the mixed economy lost some political endorsement, the goals of economic growth and expanding consumerism remained as the declared intentions of all parties, including those committed to free market and monetary policies. This made possible the acceptance of common measures in the European Economic Community.

The Russians too faced enormous tasks of reconstruction after the Second World War. They were helped by the Stalinist identification of work with pleasure, but even more by the massive use of forced labour, including deported nationalities and political prisoners. In the result, even some western economists were impressed in 1953 by a phenomenal rate of industrial growth. In this there was no concession to raising living standards, however, and no scope for radical politicians and reforming trade unions to demand them. After the death of Stalin, nevertheless, questions began to be asked about the priority given to heavy industry as opposed to the consumer industries, and in 1964 his successor Khrushchev was speaking openly of giving consumer goods top priority. For a time at least, a commitment to increased consumption with economic growth was maintained. Gorbachev attempted in his turn to switch the emphasis to the improvement of living standards and to long-neglected welfare and medical provisions. The grip of the party bureaucracy slowly loosened and increasing knowledge of standards in western Europe sharpened the appetite for economic reform.

In the Soviet satellite states in eastern Europe, the trend had not been very different. Soon after the war, in reaction to the western Marshall Plan for large-scale US aid to war-ravaged countries, an organization was set up to bring about cooperation and specialization, and trade in the bloc increased considerably as a result. Its bilateral nature was a severe limiting factor, however, and kept trade with the rest of the world at a very low level. When imports to sustain economic growth could no longer be wholly financed by exports of raw materials and manufactures, substantial credits were obtained from western banks. To help service the loans, the levels of consumption were reduced, producing unrest that was a contributory factor in attempts to replace rigid Soviet controls by a move towards a free market. Not until the withdrawal of Russian troops in the Gorbachev reforms did this prove possible, however, as a repressed desire was released to emulate western European living standards.

In China after the death of Mao, as in Russia after the death of Stalin, there was a slow change, allowing some scope for the consumer to benefit. Economic policy, even in the late 1970s, continued to follow the Soviet principle that the way to industrialize was to invest as much as possible and consume as little as possible. Believing that heavy industry would build a future, while consumer goods would delay it, the Chinese put nearly a third of their national income into industrial investment. In 1979, however, their planning strategy made a basic shift in which consumer goods, initially for export, were given a recognized place, and after 1984 central controls were modified in favour of local initiatives stressing consumer industries. To some observers, it appeared that China was creating a capitalist economy, restoring the market mechanism in allocating resources, reinstating profit as a yardstick and expanding the role of prices. In this the consumer stood to benefit.

Central planning remained, but for the thousand million or more Chinese living on the mainland the opportunities for individual advance had improved. Although still a poor country by western standards, China's industrial productivity was twice as high as India's and the appetite for improved technology was growing. At the same time, in response to consumer demand, the planners sought to widen the range of choice. In particular, acute shortages of some products were to be tackled, and unsaleable stockpiles of other goods checked, by allowing a larger role to market forces. At factory level, the income of workers was to be more closely related to the performance of their enterprises, which were themselves given more latitude in the marketing of output in excess of quotas.

For much of Islam, involvement in world markets has been crucial since the opening up of oil fields in the Middle East early in the postwar period. Government revenues soared, allowing social services to be extended in elaborate new structures of administration. By 1980 the main oil-producing states were occupying a crucial position in global markets, sharing control with the multinationals and using their bargaining power to influence prices and production. Surplus resources were invested in the industrial countries, which in return supplied capital goods and technical expertise.

By the 1960s, it became apparent that the world economy was growing at an unprecedented rate. The output of manufactures quadrupled between the early 1950s and the early 1970s, thus overtaking the losses of the war years. Even more significantly, world trade in manufactures grew tenfold as market mechanisms were restored and improved. The progress of technology was leading to larger and larger companies, practising economies of scale, using long-term planning and applying global investment strategies. The leading American companies developed into multinationals and were followed in this by the Japanese as well as the western Europeans. Their size and geographical spread put them beyond the control of individual governments as their operations drew more and more local economies, particularly in Asia, into their net. In this global marketplace, aspirations for higher living standards spread from the industrial countries into all the areas penetrated by the new financial imperialism. Resulting problems, such as inflationary pressures, inequality of incomes and ecological damage, raised doubts but appeared unlikely to check significantly the now near universal commitment to economic growth and higher living standards.

The world economy which resulted from western expansion was beginning to assume a definitive form in the twentieth century. The world economic depression of the early 1930s demonstrated (though in a wholly negative sense) that a worldwide system had come into existence; and the dominant position of the American economy after 1945 was exercised on a global scale. During the next half-century, economic goals in virtually all regions began to converge around the concepts of continuing growth and consumer betterment, whether by market forces or some form of state planning. A global marketplace had emerged, independent of political frontiers and rival ideologies. But although the existence of a world economy had indicated the possibility of a global civilization, the hostile encounters of the last hundred years had revealed a chronic failure to integrate the political systems.

17

Hostile Encounters

Civilizations at War

The hundred years of war between 1850 and 1950 originated in the rival aspirations of the western European nation-states, but as a consequence of their leading role in the world economy they assumed the proportions of world wars in the first half of the twentieth century. The inflammatory ideology of nationalism left in the residue of the French revolutionary wars not only brought the nation-states into conflict: associated with ideas of economic progress, and backed with superior technologies, it spread across the political frontiers to challenge the traditional orthodoxies of Islam, Russia and China and give additional impetus to the Japanese. Military intervention by the western Europeans contributed to internal instability as the other early modern civilizations faltered, involving them all in what became global hostile encounters.

Doctrines about the role of the state, the freedom of the individual, the tensions between them and the resort to violence to resolve them were beginning to push aside the older faiths, both in western Europe and its empires and in societies where the other early modern civilizations had prevailed. In western Europe itself nationalism and class conflict set the agenda for political change. In Russia the autocratic tsars and their advisers resorted to political police and censorship in attempts to Russianize the regions and promote panslavism. In the dismembered states of Islam fundamentalist convictions fought a rearguard action against modernization and westernization. Chinese rulers lost control of the provinces and fell victim to revolutionary doctrines, internal unrest and foreign intrusion. As the confrontations within and between the civilizations became more frequent and less easily contained, the attention given to ideological prescriptions acquired greater commitment.

For a time in the first half of the nineteenth century, the balance and the concert of powers appeared to be holding the peace. In the second half, the assumption became more tenuous in a series of wars involving Austria, Prussia and France. Emerging now as a sovereign state, Germany was becoming the leading industrial power and, in the last two decades of the century, was adopting a colonial policy. German philosophers assured their compatriots that the grandeur of history lay in the perpetual conflict of nations; and Bismarck, the genius of German expansionism, announced that 'iron and blood' would decide 'the great questions of the time'. The linked ideologies of nationalism and progress had thus led to dangerous contentions, between the European states and between the classes within those states. As the century came to an end, a belief in or at least a tacit acceptance of violence appeared to be the only alternative option for a civilization whose traditional values had failed to avert a rush to anarchy.

The Ottoman lands meanwhile were under pressure, either directly by seizure or occupation, or by the unsettling effect of ideas about liberty and self-determination. Awareness of the progress being made in Europe led some writers and officials to urge that Islam should follow suit. They sought to persuade a new generation of Muslims that they should adopt such ideas and could do so without harm to their own fundamental beliefs. After 1870, another generation was not so sure. Western Europe, having been held up as a model, was beginning to behave like an adversary. The stability of the provinces in Europe was further threatened by the fact that most of the population was non-Turkish, and even non-Muslim, and that it had never been wholly assimilated to the traditions of Islam. Eventually the Balkan nations merged their mutual hostilities in a league against the Turks.

The land of the Shahs was subject to the rival attentions of the Russian and British governments, who were encouraged by the internal disorders there to interfere in their own imperialist interests. From the late 1820s, Anglo-Russian rivalry in Persia, Afghanistan and central Asia took the form of 'the great game' which barely stopped short of a direct collision of arms. Towards the end of the century, discontent with the government and fear of foreign threats were being commonly expressed in feelings of religious nationalism or a desire for liberal reform. In India an attempt in 1831 to re-create an ideal Islamic empire from the Afghan frontier to Calcutta failed, and the Muslims were in retreat before British moves of annexation and penetration. A rebellion in 1857 led by Muslims united all classes and all religions against the British in what became known as the 'Indian mutiny'. With its failure, the last Mughal monarch was banished and the British assumed full responsibility for the subcontinent.

The trading wars in the mid-nineteenth century between western Europeans and the Chinese have been interpreted in different ways. For some Chinese historians they were the beginning of foreign imperialism in their country. Western historians, on the other hand, have seen them as marking the end of Chinese isolation from the global system and the beginning of revolutionary change. A particular cause of friction was the importation of opium from India, which British traders found profitable but the Chinese government opposed on social and financial grounds.

In 1839 Chinese officials confiscated all opium warehoused in the permitted port of Canton, leading to a fatal fracas and a legal dispute over the trial of British sailors. Hostilities broke out, and after a British victory the Treaty of Nanking ceded the right of British citizens to be tried in British courts and opened five more ports to British trade and residence. In 1856, seeking to extend their trading rights, the

British exploited an incident in which the Chinese boarded a ship and lowered the British flag. The French joined in, using as an excuse the murder of a missionary in the interior. Together the western powers mounted military operations and forced the signing of the treaties of Tientsin, which opened more ports and legalized the opium trade. When the Chinese refused to ratify the clauses, the Europeans resumed hostilities, captured Peking and burned the emperor's summer palace.

Following the Peking Convention of 1860 all foreign powers shared the privileges gained by any one of them. In what was known as 'the unequal treaty system', Germany, America, Russia and Japan also gained access to the China trade. The treaty ports quickly became cosmopolitan cities in which foreigners played an increasing role. They were given the right to travel in the interior, use the country's major waterways and propagate their own religions. The contrasted modes of life and behaviour between the Chinese and their uninvited guests caused feelings of hostility and humiliation. The use of force created an inferiority complex which hindered assimilation to the new climate of change. Intervention by the western powers also extended to other countries in East Asia, which were occupied and turned into colonies.

At some time during the nineteenth century most parts of China were subject to internal unrest or outright rebellion. The largest and the most organized movement was the Taiping rebellion in the south in 1851–64, which is said to have had few parallels in world history for its human and physical destructiveness. Flood and famine were widespread, allowing a militant religious movement to inspire an army of warriors which erupted northwards. An expedition to take the capital failed and poor overall planning undermined control of the countryside. The scholar–gentry class became antagonized and the rebellion lost direction and leadership. Against the background of widespread civil war, the central government also lost control over central Asia. In the 1890s, the Japanese won a series of decisive victories and enforced claims against the Chinese which profoundly disturbed the

Russians, who in their turn were defeated by the Japanese early in the next century. By then the Chinese had surrendered their economic, territorial, political and military independence to a host of predators from other civilizations.

The official response to divisive tendencies in Russia was an intensification of the policy of Russification in an atmosphere of growing intolerance. The western provinces were the most open to European ideas of nationalism and it was there that the authorities sought most ruthlessly to root out manifestations of cultural differences. With something like a hundred distinct national peoples within its borders, the Russian empire was one of the most varied in the world. In the early days, the existing apparatus of administration was often left intact, but by 1900 little local autonomy remained. Religious differences were a constant source of strife, not only among Christians but also among the millions of Jews in European Russia and the considerable communities of Muslims further south and east.

There was little in the system to provide and protect rights for individuals. Offences against the state were codified in 1832, and in 1845 a new criminal code conferred wide-ranging powers on the agents of law and order. At the end of the 1850s, and to some extent in response to the new criminal code, a revolutionary movement began to take shape. In the next two decades, the main form of radicalism was populism, devoted in various ways to the emancipation of the people. Populism was suspicious of the coming of capitalism and contemptuous of the processes of political reform. A wave of terrorism culminated in 1881 in the assassination of Tsar Alexander II on the instructions of a militant group claiming to represent 'the people'.

Early in the next century, the failure of the European balance of power unleashed a world war which brought to an end the empires of tsarist Russia, the Ottoman power and China. The war has been the subject of intense debate by historians. It has been variously interpreted as the result of accumulated tensions from the previous century, as marking a total break with the past and the beginning of a new phase of history, and as the cause of economic and social miseries, political fanaticism and terrorism, and eventually the further horrors of the second world war. In a sense it was all these things, but above all it may be seen as bringing to a head a crisis of belief. At the end of the nineteenth century, the values implicit in western European civilization which had been promoted so confidently throughout the world were still largely unchallenged. There was the belief in progress and in a continuation of economic growth and social betterment in which all might increasingly share. There was an assumption that at the root of behaviour there still lay a prevailing Christian ethic which was tolerant and humanitarian. There was an acceptance that the international rule of law could be maintained. By the end of the war, these beliefs were in profound disarray, and the claim of the western Europeans to moral and practical superiority was no longer tenable.

When the wartime collapse of the tsarist empire was followed by the communist takeover, Russian society came to be dominated by two general features: a prescriptive ideology, and the systematic use of terror to secure conformity. The use of state terror had its roots in the police state of the final decades of tsarist rule, but it far exceeded it. Lenin claimed that the party must act on behalf of the proletariat and, in its name, he assumed dictatorial powers. He declared that 'unlimited power based on violence and bound by no laws' was justified to ensure the survival of the soviet state. The despotic rule which the party exercised over Russian society – at a huge cost in life, suffering and economic deprivation – was eventually extended to its own ranks and at Stalin's behest there was a savage purge of its leadership. Marxism ceased in effect to be an independent factor in the determination of policy and became instead a ritual creed to justify a relentless tyranny.

The techniques of totalitarian rule spread quickly into western Europe in conditions of political instability and economic distress which afflicted Italy and Germany. In Italy, the bourgeoisie supported fascism as providing an end to revolutionary socialism while curbing the power of big business.

The ideology of the Nazi movement had been set out in the two volumes of *Mein Kampf*, written by Hitler in the 1920s. The first volume expressed the racist ideology of Aryan supremacy and Jewish parasites, and declared a need for Germans to gain living space in the east at the expense of the Slavs and the Russian communists. The second volume outlined a political process in which terrorist methods were to be prominent. The Italian dictator Mussolini believed that the working-class movement needed irrational myths to perform its role in history and that violence was a necessary means of countering the existing social order.

No agreed strategy emerged in the 1930s to contain or restrain the aggressive powers in Europe and Asia. In a second world war, an alliance of opposed ideologies was forced into existence by the tide of events rather than by considered rational means. Germany overran western Europe, and the Japanese began a full-scale war against China. When German armies invaded Poland, Britain and France entered the conflict. In 1941, Germany attacked Russia, Japan attacked the American Pacific fleet and launched an Asian offensive, Britain and America declared war on Japan, and Germany declared war on America. An alliance of Britain, America and Russia was now engaged globally against Japan, Germany and Italy until peace returned in 1945.

The basic reality of international relations after 1945 was the concern of the United States to protect its global economic interests, and the concern of the Soviet Union to protect its political borders. In practice, spheres of influence allowed American predominance in the capitalist world and Soviet hegemony in its satellite zone, while hot wars were prosecuted in east and south Asia and propaganda wars in the rest of the world. Military engagements in Korea and Vietnam were inconclusive for America, at a heavy cost for the native peoples and a loss of confidence and cohesion in America. After the death of Stalin in 1953, there were attempts in the satellite states to free their systems from Soviet control. These were at first suppressed by the Russians, but by 1990 the entire Soviet empire began to break up. The demolition of the Berlin Wall signalled a move towards the reunification of Germany, with an implied recasting of the security map of the whole continent.

The Chinese communists had proclaimed a People's Republic in 1949; and, faced after the long civil war with immense problems of defence, rural reclamation and industrial recovery, they turned to Moscow as the only available source of help. The 1950 treaty of friendship, alliance and mutual assistance was the result; and, for a decade, China benefited from Russian supplies and technicians. But deep differences of policy and interest between the two communist powers had by then emerged: the Russians withdrew their help and increasingly the Chinese went their own way. From the start, they attempted to transform a traditional society into something different. To this end the country was subjected to a series of radical experiments. By 1976, however, the political system, the economy and the educational structure were largely run down and lacking direction. Although, by the 1980s, the political position appeared to have stabilized, there was a feeling of outrage in 1989 when a pro-democracy movement led by students in Tiananmen Square was suppressed by an outright massacre.

Warfare was seldom absent from the Middle East, full-scale conflicts being interspersed with periods of rearmament and precarious diplomacy. Israeli occupation of Palestine led to a protracted period of hostilities. In 1956, Britain and France colluded with Israel in an attack on Egypt; and Egypt thereafter asserted Arab military leadership against Israel, notably in 1967 and 1973. In 1980, Iraq began a war with Iran which was partly religious and partly territorial. When fighting ended eight years later, the Arab world had been divided. In 1990–1, Iraq's invasion of the oil-rich sheikdom of Kuwait was reversed after intervention by the United Nations, with the technically superior United States leading an international coalition. It included most Arab states and was supported militarily by the western Europeans and financially by the Japanese, with the Russians mostly on the sidelines.

Thus ended a century of hostile encounters between the civilizations, in which political structures and safeguards were tested and found wanting. In one sense, the encounters and the wars were an expression of the limitations reached by the modern regional empires. In another sense, they represented attempts to find a political settlement to sustain the economic foundation of a new global system. Although they also failed in this, the two world wars bequeathed to later generations the means to a global network of communications. This network and its global implications are the subject of the final chapter.

18

Communication Network

Search for Coexistence

Political events in the twentieth century have had a direct impact on economic developments, not least in the technology of modern warfare and in land, sea and air transport. The continental ambitions of Germany and America focused early attention on land transport, and the Anglo-German arms race stimulated naval construction. Wartime advances in combat aircraft were followed by commercial aviation to link overseas territories. The second world war brought further technical innovation, leading to jet-propelled flight and earth satellites and a massive growth of commercial airlines. Nuclear research to produce an atom bomb revolutionized the technology of weaponry and affected all fields of transportation, communications and power generation in what became known as the 'military-industrial complex'. The wartime challenges had also stimulated computer advances, which, allied to developments in electronics, transformed global communications. The relationship between these political events, the technological innovations, and the prevailing belief systems, was complex and continuous, providing the leading themes of later twentieth-century history.

While the maritime powers of western Europe had been creating empires across the seas, the states of central Europe had remained divided and provincial. In the nineteenth century this situation had been transformed: by political unification, by industrial revolution and by military initiative. Under Prussian leadership, ambitions were formed to revise the existing territorial order. A reform of military recruitment gave the Germans a proportionately far larger front-line army, and the chief of staff von Moltke used the railways to mobilize and move it into action, while the telegraph enabled field orders to be issued from military headquarters. In the war against Austria in 1866 and against France in 1871 this strategy gave the Germans the decisive advantage. At about the same time, German engineers made the crucial inventions which led to the internal combustion engine and the revolution in road transport. Gottlieb Daimler was building vehicles propelled by petrol engines, and in 1885 Karl Benz applied the invention specifically to motor cars.

For the rapid further development of motor transport, three things were necessary: ready availability of petrol, ample space for motor roads, and new industrial techniques to provide cheap cars for a mass market. All these were present in the United States, and having completed the drive to the Pacific, the country needed fast and convenient transport for a coast-to-coast society of growing farms and townships. On the eastern seaboard of America, where the railways were mainly concentrated, populous cities were expanding, and to the west movement of settlers into virgin lands offered scope for new-style communications. America also had oil: in Pennsylvania, in mid-continent, in California and on the Gulf coast. By 1918 all were on stream and output was nearly six times what it had been in 1900. Meantime America had solved the problem of the cheap motor car, with industrial innovations which were to have profound repercussions in manufacturing everywhere and on the wealth and importance of the United States. In the second decade of the century, Henry Ford in Detroit applied the assembly-line method of production to a car designed for the mass consumer market.

The lead in warship design was retained by the British from the early years of the century by the Dreadnought, whose big-gun armament made previous designs obsolescent, leading to the final phase of the shipbuilding race with Germany in the run-up to the first world war. The nineteenth century had seen the transition from sail to steam and from wood to steel, with comparable advances in gunnery. In anticipation of war breaking out between them, the nation-states made a rapid transfer to steam turbines for their largest and most heavily armed ships. In the last decade of the century, naval rivalry between Britain and Germany became particularly intense, with political and economic conse-quences. In a separate development, the tanker was pioneered by the Germans for the transport of oil, stimulated by the new mass market for motor cars.

The German imperial wars were also decisive in stimulat-ing the air transport revolution. Only a decade before the first world war, the Wright brothers in America had demonstrated the possibility of powered flight in a vehicle that was heavier than air and used a petrol engine. The military possibilities were explored and air rivalry brought a series of technical advances in combat aircraft. The most formidable aircraft of the period were the German Zeppelins, huge metal-framed airships carrying high explosive and incendiary bombs. The most important work, however, was in reconnaissance over enemy lines, gathering intelligence and testing strategic con-cepts. Commercial aviation followed soon after the war, when the imperial powers introduced air routes to serve their overseas territories. By the early 1930s, converted bombers had been largely replaced by aircraft designed primarily for the handling of passengers and cargo.

The Second World War brought further technical innova-tion on both sides of the conflict, including the introduction of an effective long-range fighter and of heavy precision bombing. The possibility of a gas turbine engine had been recognized in Britain by Frank Whittle in 1930, but it was not until the approach of war that a research team was estab-lished. It was the Germans who introduced jets into active service during the war. By the end of the war, both countries were operating jet designs, which were adopted for most military uses because of their greater speed and power. The Germans broke new ground in rocketry, providing a basis for jet-propelled flight and earth-orbiting satellites after the war.

The first artificial satellite was launched by Soviet Russia in 1957, prompting the United States to accelerate its own space programme and land the first man on the moon in 1969. Commercial aviation meantime was expanding rapidly on a global basis. The first jet aeroplane to appear on commercial routes was the British de Havilland Comet, which began service in 1952, and the Americans followed with the Boeing 707 by the end of the decade. The cost of research encouraged some international cooperation, as in the British-French Concorde aircraft in 1970. An immense outlay on airport building was undertaken worldwide from then on to meet the demand for commercial and tourist traffic.

On the heels of the transport revolution came the transformation of other kinds of communication. The electric telegraph, which had been effective in nineteenth-century wars, also brought European business communities into instantaneous contact. The laying of transoceanic cables from around 1870 created the beginnings of a global system, with messages transmitted by Morse code, which had been pioneered in the United States. It was also in America that the first commercial telephone system was installed following inventions by Alexander Bell. From experiments in Germany, the linking of electric current to a transmitting circuit made radio communication possible and in 1901 the first wireless signal was sent across the Atlantic by Marconi. The thermionic valve introduced the age of amplified and rectified signals, so that voices could be sent across the air waves and received on wireless radio sets. Cinemas were showing silent films from the beginning of the century and talking films from the 1930s, by which time television had been introduced.

The first indication that an atomic bomb could be built was given by two British professors in February 1940. Further research was put in hand at Oxford University and, by mid-1941, it was becoming clear that large-scale research work would be needed and that only in America were the necessary production resources available. Until 1942 the American research effort had been less intense and less successful, but after US entry into the war expenditure was massively increased, leading to the testing of a plutonium weapon in New Mexico in July 1945. In the following month atom bombs were dropped on two Japanese cities, bringing an end to the Second World War and bequeathing an age of nuclear terror worldwide. The new nuclear weapons revolutionized the military situation and the pace of development accelerated beyond anything previously known. Atomic bombs boosted destructive power two thousand times, and within ten years the thermonuclear bomb had multiplied it a thousand times more. Within the same period long-range bombers brought the main world centres of power and production within reach of each other and intercontinental missiles appeared on the scene. To detect the potential of a prospective enemy it became important to make observations from space and artificial satellites were used for this purpose.

The growth of the weapons industry after 1945 led the US President Eisenhower to warn in his farewell address in 1961 that 'an immense military establishment and a large arms industry' – a military-industrial complex – might continue to poison the wells of international relations and to dominate domestic policy. The export of arms had become crucial to some of the advanced nations, which traded arms for oil in the Middle East and encouraged third world countries to buy weapons instead of food or welfare. The spin-off from arms manufacture into virtually all fields of transportation, communication and power generation made its impact so continuous and far-reaching that realistic dividing lines between military and civilian production could no longer be drawn.

In the development of satellites, the revolution in transport systems was linked with the parallel revolution in communications associated with computer technology and automated processes in industry. The first generation of computers was used mainly by scientists and technologists, who needed faster and more versatile methods of solving problems in applied mathematics. Of crucial importance to computer theory and the logical analysis of computer processes was the work of Alan Turing in cracking the German Enigma code at the British code and cipher school. The first computer using electronics was built for the US Army at the end of the war for calculating trajectories and firing tables. By 1955 the first commercial computers had come into operation and they began to look like big business. By 1959 the thermionic valve had been replaced by the transistor, based on discoveries in the Bell Telephone laboratory: this led to the second generation of computers and transformed the design and manufacture of radio and television sets. The 1960s saw the link-up between satellites in space and television transmission, the introduction of microcircuits into computers, and confident prophecies of further applications.

The artificial satellite Telstar was put into orbit to serve as a radio relay line between America and Europe, and in 1962 it was used for a television tie-up. Three years later it was followed by Early Bird, the first of a series designed to provide worldwide coverage. At about this time microelectronics was being developed commercially in America. Microphotographic methods were used to create large numbers of electronic circuits on the surface of small fragments of silicon. These could be manufactured in large quantities at small cost, with high reliability and long durability, ushering in a new era of information transmission. The storage of vast amounts of data on magnetized tape or disk and instantaneous interchange between widely separate systems of information pointed the way to a global internet of incalculable possibilities.

The use of nuclear energy for peaceful purposes also held out exceptional promise, but not without problems. From the 1950s, atomic power stations were added to the electricity generation grids in Europe, America and Russia and in several third world countries. The great advantages of nuclear fuel were in avoiding atmospheric pollution and in offering an alternative to fossil fuels, which were likely eventually to run out. There were, however, doubts about the safety and reliability of atomic power stations in operation and about the disposal of radioactive waste. A series of accidents and a lack of agreement about waste cast a shadow over the future of nuclear energy, but nevertheless it continued to attract plans and research for further ongoing development.

The growth of multinational corporations in the 1960s and 1970s indicated a shift towards global financial systems based in America, Europe and Japan, but acting independently of the political structure. The development of fast and frequent air travel, of world telephone and telex tie-ups, and of new electronic computers to handle masses of information at high speed had made it possible for a spread of subsidiaries across the globe to be continuously subject to central strategic planning. By the end of the twentieth century, the shape of a globalizing economy was beginning to emerge. Among the many networks through which it operated were an international money exchange which handled vast sums every day in virtually every currency; an international marketplace in which goods and materials and services were traded around the world; and an international factory of plants, offices and contracts, with their own banks of information and communication links. This economy, on a scale greatly exceeding that of any national economy or political empire and largely beyond the control of any nominally sovereign state, directly affected everybody in the industrial world and indirectly affected billions more outside it.

The world economy which had been evolving since the sixteenth century now had at its disposal the most powerful and comprehensive network of communications since the first global odyssey, a potential for political cooperation on a global scale. By the end of the twentieth century, attempts at global political structures had not evolved to a comparable extent, however. The nineteenth-century international order collapsed into two world wars, out of which came first the League of Nations and secondly the United Nations to promote cooperation and avoid armed conflict between the sovereign states. In practice, the United States became the most formidable player in the world economy, but by the end of the century control of the world order was beyond the reach of any single state or group of states. By then all nation-states were obliged to recognize that international capital and multinational production facilities constituted a global capacity beyond their control, to whose pressures they were forced to react.

The human species which set out on a global odyssey a hundred thousand years ago had inherited the earth. Every acre of land is now claimed, owned or controlled by individuals or by nation-states or by corporate bodies. Some is still being contested or fought over, even as categories of use are being assigned and debated. The moving frontier is reaching a terminus, as the number of human occupants of the globe reaches 6 billion and goes on growing. The ratio between productive soil and human need has become critical in many regions. Agricultural expansion and depletion of forests and grasslands was greater in the thirty years from 1950 than in the 150 years from 1700, and human impact has caused and is causing lasting damage.

Global history began with the search for suitable habitats yielding an adequate subsistence. In the transition many millennia later to civilized centres, surpluses above subsistence were needed to provide for more permanent and complex societies. The carrying capacity of the earth was again dramatically increased by the industrial revolution of two centuries ago and the consequential creation of a world economic system. The industrial age appears now to be passing into a new technological age, based on electronic sectors and advances in biochemicals to raise the productivity of the soil. Questions are being raised whether the momentum is sustainable without global environmental disruption or major social disorder.

Against this background new areas of debate have focused on the relationship between organisms and their environment and on the extension and impact of human societies. Ecology has entered the agenda of biologists, sociologists and historians in a series of studies identifying some interdisciplinary themes of global history. At one end of the debate are the plagues and diseases which threatened the classical empires, retarded European development in the fourteenth century and accelerated the demise of Amerindian civilizations in the sixteenth.[1] On the more positive side were the crossing of biological boundary lines, when plants were transposed by Islamic traders and farmers which speeded the creation of a new modern civilization.[2] The process also enabled Europeans to transplant their civilization to widely spaced temperate zones across the world more by biological means than military.[3] Human interactions with the environment via technologies have opened up an academic field of interest that extends from stone tools through steam engines to the internet.[4] They currently raise issues of acute concern such as global warming, nuclear armaments, recurrent famine and flooding, and new infectious diseases.[5]

Global tendencies

In the last two centuries the outlines of a world economic system have emerged, superimposed on a politically and ideo-logically divided world. The period has been variously char-acterized as an age of ideology, of increasingly global conflict, and as a revolution in the technology of communications. Through a century of hostile encounters, fuelled by European rivalries and pushing imperial systems into terminal decline, attempts at improved political cooperation have been made, while religious, ethnic and nationalist conflict has intensified.

Through the nineteenth century the goals of nationalism and liberal democracy were in competition throughout Europe, sharpening in the twentieth century into totalitarian doctrines and versions of welfare economics, and into the industrialization of conflict in two world wars. The idea of socialism reached more of humankind than any world reli-gion, while the realities of capitalism survived economic crisis to challenge communism in the period of the Cold War. Focused on the global strategies of America and the Soviet Union, the Cold War drew China, Europe, Islam and the uncommitted nations into an unstable and threatening complex. Meanwhile economic power centres across the

Atlantic and round the Pacific rim entered into a global arena of multinational finance in which techniques of information access affected virtually all regions of the world.

It is tempting to see in these circumstances similarities with what occurred at the end of the classical era. Political boundaries had eroded with the passing of the empires, competing ideologies were reaching beyond them in global tendencies, and new information systems were providing for communication across the regions. The knowledge of production techniques and political processes had not been lost and could be restored and extended when conditions of stability returned in areas favourable to economic growth. This, as always, was where new civilized centres could begin to form, using old and new channels of exchange to enlarge the scope for material well-being and encourage an eventual impetus towards political cooperation.

NOTES

1   W. H. McNeill, *Plagues and Peoples*, Blackwell, 1977.
2   A. M. Watson, *Agricultural Innovation in the Early Islamic World*, Cambridge University Press, 1983.
3   A. W. Crosby, *Ecological Imperialism*, Cambridge University Press, 1986.
4   J. Diamond, *Guns, Germs and Steel*, Cape, 1997.
5   A. King and B. Schneider, *The First Global Revolution*, Simon and Schuster, 1991.

Conclusion

Civilization and globalization

The interacting themes of this book have been civilization and globalization. The former is a familiar term in the writing of history, the latter a more recent expression whose nature and significance are still being debated and defined. I have used these terms to indicate two persistent trends in the human experience: the impulse towards permanent settlement and the impulse towards wider horizons. While at first there appears to be a tension between these impulses, a major outcome of this study is a growing understanding of their interrelatedness. Although all the civilizations were based on the achievement of permanent settlement, the very success of some permanent settlements led to a sequence of expansionary pressures of an economic, political and ideological nature. These pressures combined to produce what may be called a global tendency at work in all the civilizations studied.

Economic pressures

The economic expansionary pressures of settler societies arose from their basic need for a surplus over subsistence, for without a surplus the continuing demand for the apparatus of permanence could not be met. Despite the favourable nature of the chosen habitats, some materials had to be brought in from outside, involving prospecting and the protection of supply routes. The very success of this process was a stimulus to population growth, which in turn increased the demand for imported supplies. Sooner or later the search for extra sources brought the settlers into contact with other communities, and new relationships developed, either by way of peaceful trading or by more predatory habits. At some levels of population, stable systems of exchange could benefit both sides. But the internal pressures of population growth and the external pressures of nomadic societies created a need for more permanent arrangements. Alongside the economic factor a political factor was increasing in importance.

Political problems

This was nothing new to the settlers, whose complex lifestyle had involved patterns of organization for the control of land and water, for the division of labour, for the distribution of rations, for the planning of expeditions, and so forth. The enlargement of these practices to include other societies called for some political accommodation between them, preferably peaceful but if necessary by force of arms. Nomadic societies by necessity had different social arrangements, arising from the different requirements of a pastoral economy. It is likely that in the early days of expanding settlements some attempts to resolve the problems of adjustment will have failed. Over longer periods and wider areas, more lasting and effective political arrangements prevailed. The most successful were the ones that preserved the different interests of settled peoples and those practising a still partly mobile existence. From an expanding political core, zones of increasing influence and control spread outwards along the corridors of trade and tribute, reinforced over time first by military measures and eventually by civil administration. To the economic impulse to expand the boundaries had been added the political requirement to define and defend the growing hegemonies. Its final expression came in the political empires across the regions, which persisted with many ups and downs over the millennia.

The belief factor

A third factor which would contribute to a slowly emerging global tendency lay in the belief systems which had held the settled societies together in their economic tasks and their political needs. Encouraged and manipulated by ruling elites in the interests of social conformity, such belief systems took on the double role of maintaining internal security while inducing commitment and support from the outer communities. Alongside the economic structure of commercial activities and the political structure of enhanced connections and control, there grew parallel patterns of commitment based on common beliefs and aspirations. Acquiring in time their own access to economic resources and political influences, they gained an independence of aims and methods which enabled them to survive the breakdown of the empires and transcend political boundaries. Behind the globalizing tendency of economic and political systems there was now the third input of belief systems involving an impetus towards conversion not limited by political boundaries. Forming their own institutional framework in the shape of would-be universal churches, they contributed to a global tendency which outlasted the civilizations in whose sequences it had persistently appeared.

Phases and factors

This study has followed the classical civilizations from their beginnings through growth and into periods of political failure and crises of belief. After an interval there were new beginnings in what became the early modern civilizations. Still later, and drawing on their experience, came the civilizations of modern America and Japan. By analysing these civilizations in terms of the core problems of economics, politics and belief, it has been possible to reveal parallel developments so that new insights are allowed into these civilized regions. It has also become possible to compare and contrast civilizations widely separated by time as well as place. Sumerian society, for example, five millennia ago and American society in the last four centuries can be analysed alongside each other in terms of the sequence of problems that each has faced and the shifting relationship between economics, politics and belief. In both of them, and in all the civilizations in between, there are clues to assessing the direction of the global tendency now shaping our lives. Across the millennia from Eurasia to the Americas, the tension between the conflicting but ultimately complementary impulses, to stay settled and to move on, has nurtured a tendency which has appeared in our own time in global transformations, affecting how we work, how we organize and how we look for meaning beyond the here and now. The same three factors of living together which confronted the first settlers and informed their encounters with other societies are present in a perplexing array across the emerging global experience. It is too early to talk confidently, or indeed meaningfully, about a global system, a global society. We are still at the stage of global tendencies. If the outlines of a possible global economy are vaguely in sight, we are only just beginning to grasp the implications of a global political system to reconcile the competing and often anarchic relations between power centres. In itself even that would not be enough, indeed would be unlikely to happen, unless over and above the limits of localized creeds and ideologies a common purpose could create the will to make and sustain an international order.

Bibliography

A note on sources A global history bibliography could fill a book. My intention is more modest and I hope more practical. It is to give a broad indication of the available literature, with particular attention to the last two decades. During this period books have begun to appear that deal with the parameters of the human experience, our early beginnings and our latest global tendencies. Histories of civilizations, which were popular when I started my research, now appear less often, and the current focus is more on connections between them. Both categories are relevant to this study and I have also included some early titles which are still useful.

The bibliography is annotated and is in six parts, as in the order of contents. In each part I have listed first the books most useful for the development of my basic themes. The order follows the sequence of the chapters. There then follow some additional sources (listed alphabetically) which either provide general background or contain material of particular relevance.

I The Primary Concern

Mellars, P. and Stringer, C., eds, *The Human Revolution*, 1989.
All aspects of the origins and dispersal of biologically modern human populations, and the development of behavioural patterns, including social change, language and related tool types.
Gebauer, A.B. and Price, T.D., eds, *Transitions to Agriculture in Prehistory*, 1992.
The simultaneous appearance and spread of domesticated plants and animals in many different areas of the world, involving long-term changes in the structures of societies and their relationship with the environment.

Snooks, J.P., *The Dynamic Society*, 1996.
Wide-ranging attempt to explore the sources of global change in a competitive environment. Focused on the dominant strategy of family multiplication and the supporting strategies of technology, commerce and conquest.
Gowlett, J.A.J., *Ascent to Civilisation*, 1993.
The archaeology of early humans. Essential handbook, clearly illustrated with diagrams and charts, showing the rise and development of human culture in all the continents.
Maisels, C.R., *The Emergence of Civilisations*, 1993.
The appearance of settlements, before and during cultivation, showing the crystallization of the village as a type, leading to city genesis and the state. Focused on the Near East.
McNeill, W.H. and Sedlar, J.W., *The Ancient Near East*, 1968.
Readings from the myths and customs of Egypt and Mesopotamia, illustrating the integration of government along with belief in a uniformity of viewpoint.

Additional sources

Adams, R.M., *The Evolution of Urban Society*, 1965.
Early Mesopotamia and prehistoric Mexico compared. Useful study of subsistence, settlement and surplus.
Burney, C., *From Village to Empire*, 1977.
An introduction to Near Eastern archaeology, sites and sequences.
Coe, M.D., *Mexico from the Olmecs to the Aztecs*, 1994.
Latest edition of a standard work on Mesoamerican civilization.
Davidson, B., *Africa in History*, 1984.
A chronological account of developments throughout the continent.
Kingdom, J., *Self-Made Man*, 1993.
Dispersal and subsistence from African origins into all the continents.
Leakey, R., *The Origin of Mankind*, 1995.
Popular introduction, taking in art and language.
Megarry, T., *Society in Prehistory*, 1995.
Origins of human culture as seen by a sociologist.
Moseley, M.E., *The Incas and their Ancestors*, 1992.
The main phases of development in the Andean region of south America.
Roberts, N., *The Holocene*, 1989.
Relationship between people and nature during the last 10,000 years.
Stringer, C. and Gamble, C., *African Exodus*, 1996.
Argues the case for an African genesis for modern humanity.

II The Political Prospect

Khazonov, A.M., *Nomads and the Outside World*, 1984.
An innovatory study of the nomadic lifestyle and its impact on sedentary societies of Afro-Eurasia.

Barfield, T.J., *The Perilous Frontier*, 1989.
The impact of nomadic empires on China from 221 BC; showing influence in both directions and introducing the horse chariot.
Hodges, H., *Technology in the Ancient World*, 1970.
Useful introduction, covering the early dynasties, chariots and ships, Greeks and Persians, and the barbarians in the West.
Horrocks, G., *Greek: a History of the Language and its Speakers*, 1997.
Detailed study of a crucial element in the network of communication in the Hellenistic world, the Roman empire, and Byzantium.
Boardman, J., Griffin, J. and Murray, O., eds, *The Oxford History of the Classical World*, 1986.
Greek, Hellenistic and Roman history and civilization, political and social etc., from the eighth century BC.
Milston, G., *A Short History of China*, 1978.
Early history and empires, invasions and migrations, recentralization of government from the early Tang period.
Thapur, R., *A History of India*, 1966.
Economic and social developments within a political structure, Mauryan and Gupta regimes, invasions and conflict.
Mann, M., *The Sources of Social Power*, vol. 1, 1986.
Early civilizations and empires, nomadic intrusions; economic and political organization.

Additional sources

Andrewes, A., *The Greeks*, 1972.
Political history, commerce, colonization, coinage, Athenian leadership.
Bowman, A.K., *Egypt after the Pharaohs*, 1986.
A period of invasion from Alexander through the Greco-Roman centuries to the coming of Islam.
Frank, A.G., *The Centrality of Central Asia*, 1992.
Interactions with outlying peoples and civilizations from nomadic and semi-sedentary bases.
Katz, F., *The Ancient American Civilisations*, 1969.
Parallel treatment of Mesoamerica and Peru, showing convulsions leading to Maya decline and Aztec hegemony.
Keay, J., *India: a History*, 2000.
Inward incursion and outward dissemination of Indian culture.
Mallory, J.P., *In Search of the Indo-Europeans*, 1989.
Language, archaeology and myth in massive movements across Eurasia from India to northern Europe.
Mukerjee, R., *The Culture and Art of India*, 1959.
The continuity of Indian civilization through struggle and assimilation.

Needham, J., *The Shorter Science and Civilisation in China*, vol. 3, abridged by C. A. Ronan, 1986.
Maritime history and technology, the compass, oceanic exploration.
Oates, J., *Babylon*, 1986.
The rise and decay of Babylonian eminence, and final abandonment.
Pirenne, J., *The Tides of History*, vol. 1, 1956.
Periodic invasions of civilized centres in the Middle East, Egypt and the Mediterranean.
Renfrew, C., *Archaeology and Language*, 1987.
An attempted synthesis of modern historical linguistics and cultural archaeology across Eurasia.
Saggs, H. W. F., *The Might that was Assyria*, 1984.
The creation of a single power structure from Iran to Egypt, overriding ethnic barriers.
Walbank, F. W., *The Hellenistic World*, 1993.
The sequel to Alexander's conquests, separate kingdoms linked by Greek language and culture.

III   The Religious Factor

Jaspers, K., *The Origins and Goal of History*, 1953.
First millennium BC seen as the watershed of history, an 'axial age' when independently in China, India, Persia, Israel and Greece world religions emerged.
Ling, T., *A History of Religion East and West*, 1968.
Includes Zoroastrianism, Judaism, Christianity, Buddhism, Brahmanism, Confucianism, etc., in a comparative historical account.
Mirsky, J., *Houses of God*, 1966.
Temples, churches and other religious buildings in Buddhism, Hinduism, the Greco-Roman world, Judaism and Christianity; religious concepts and architectural motifs.
Bentley, J. H., *Old World Encounters*, 1993.
Cross-cultural contacts and exchanges in premodern times: conversion, conflict and compromise.
Zaehner, R. C., *The Dawn and Twilight of Zoroastrianism*, 1961.
Historical phases of the Persian religion, showing its intimate relation to dynastic and political change.
Whiting, P., *Byzantium: an Introduction*, 1981.
Religion and politics in the eastern Roman empire from the time of Constantine.
Brown, P., *The World of Late Antiquity*, 1971.
Society and religion in east and west Europe and the Near East after the conflict and end of the empires.

Additional sources

Chan, W.-T., *A Source Book of Chinese Philosophy*, 1963.
A historical perspective of Confucianist and Buddhist thought.
Chandhuri, N.C., *Hinduism*, 1979.
A historical description and analytical account.
Croix, G.E.M., de S., *The Class Struggle in the Ancient Greek World*, 1981.
Political and religious trends on a broad compass.
Epstein, I., *Judaism: a Historical Presentation*, 1959.
Origin and development of religion and ethics.
Grant, M., *The World of Rome*, 1960.
State and society and beliefs in the empire.
Herrin, J., *The Formation of Christendom*, 1987.
From late antiquity, schism and division.
Humphreys, C., *Buddhism*, 1951.
History and development of the various schools.
Needham, J., *Science and Civilisation in China*, vol. 2, 1956.
History of scientific thought in the main religious traditions.
Nigosian, S.A., *World Faiths*, 1994.
Historical background and beliefs of the separate traditions.
Radhakrishnan, S. and Moore, C.H., *A Source Book in Indian Philosophy*, 1967.
From the Vedic and Epic periods to Buddhism.

IV   New Beginnings

Anderson, P., *Passages from Antiquity to Feudalism*, 1978.
Nomadic invasions of eastern and western Europe, shifting the focus from the Mediterranean world to a new economic dynamic.
Jones, G., *A History of the Vikings*, 1968.
The penetration of western Europe, the Slav and Muslim worlds and Byzantium by means of warfare, trade and colonization.
Singer, C., Holmyard, E.J., Hall A.R. and Williams, T.I., *A History of Technology*, vol. 2, 1956.
The shifting emphasis from Mediterranean civilization to the north-west, laying the basis for new technology.
Gimpel, J., *The Medieval Machine*, 1998.
The industrial revolution of the Middle Ages, following the impact on agriculture of new sources of energy and three-field rotation.
Watson, A.M., *Agricultural Innovation in the Early Islamic World*, 1983.
The diffusion of crops and farming techniques 700–1100. Pathways and mechanics of an agricultural revolution.

Gernet, J., *A History of Chinese Civilisation*, 1982.
Treats the emergence of the 'Chinese Middle Ages', characterized by ethnic and agrarian change, expansion of rice growing, commerce and new industries.
Dukes, P., *A History of Russia*, 1974.
Treats medieval economic development, including agricultural expansion and participation in international trade using forest products; Christianity as state religion.

Additional sources

Ashtor, E., *A Social and Economic History of the Near East in the Middle Ages*, 1976.
Major changes in the social framework in support of economic change.
Bartlett, R., *The Making of Europe*, 1993.
The expansion of Latin Christendom, including the balance of political power and the significance of the Roman church.
Benson, R.L. and Constable, G.L., eds, *Renaissance and Renewal in the Twelfth Century*, 1991.
Religion, society and culture, politics, philosophy and science, in a receptive response to the coming of a new world.
Dawson, R., *Imperial China*, 1972.
The departures from classical culture, reunification, economic advance.
Frye, R.N., *The Golden Age of Persia*, 1975.
The Arabs in the east, conquests and consequences, the Islamic ecumene.
Kazhdan, A.P. and Epstein, A.W., *Change in Byzantine Culture in the Eleventh and Twelfth Centuries*, 1985.
Dynamic social changes as part of the political, economic and intellectual fabric.
Koenigsberger, H.G., *Medieval Europe 400–1500*, 1987.
New and distinctive European identity manifested in social, political, economic and cultural issues.
McNeill, W.H., *Plagues and Peoples*, 1977.
The role of pestilence in human history.
Milner-Gulland, R. and Dejevsky, N., *Atlas of Russia and the Soviet Union*, 1989.
From Kievan state to Muscovy, land and people, the tsars and the patriarchs.
Pipes, R., *Russia under the Old Regime*, 1974.
The patrimonial regime, ecclesiastical submission, agricultural poverty.

V Wider Identities

Parry, J.H., *The Age of Reconnaisance*, 1963.
European exploration, trade and settlement in other continents, from conditions to consequences.

Auty, R. and Obolensky, D., *An Introduction to Russian History*, 1976.
Territorial expansion in the south and east incorporating non-European and non-Christian peoples, exploitation of resources by Peter and Catherine, westernization v. tradition.

Hodgson, M.G.S., *The Venture of Islam*, vol. 3: *The Gunpowder Empires and Modern Times*, 1974.
Extensive political and cultural renewal from which emerged the Safavi, Indian and Ottoman empires; developments in the Islamic ecumene.

Fairbank, J.K., *China: a New History*, 1992.
Comprehensive survey, particularly useful on the Mongol empire, Ming ambitions, Manchu conquest and control in inner Asia. Territorial administration through military organization.

Deane, P., *The First Industrial Revolution*, 1969.
Systematic treatment of all the factors in Britain's early lead, using concepts and techniques of development economics.

Stearns, P.N., *The Industrial Revolution in World History*, 1993.
The spread of rapid industrialization in western Europe and the United States, the expansion of railroads and heavy industry in Germany and the US, growing involvement elsewhere.

Headrick, D.R., *The Tools of Empire*, 1981.
Imperialism and technology in the nineteenth century: penetration, conquests, communications.

Joll, J., *Europe since 1870*, 1976.
Socialism, liberalism, imperialism, against an international political background.

Hourani, A., *Arabic Thought in the Liberal Age, 1798–1939*, 1983.
Modernizing trend of political and social thought in the Arab Middle East.

Gray, J., *Rebellions and Revolutions: China from the 1800s*, 1990.
The traditional society and conflict with the western powers.

Additional sources

Cook, M.A., ed., *A History of the Ottoman Empire to 1730*, 1976.
The origins and early growth of the Muslim state in Europe.

Davis, R., *The Rise of the Atlantic Economies*, 1973.
Integrated study of the economic history of societies on both sides of the Atlantic.

Ferro, M., *Colonisation: a Global History*, 1997.
Comprehensive coverage, emphasizing social and cultural aspects and new types of economies.

Hartwell, R.M., *The Industrial Revolution and Economic Growth*, 1971.
Causes and process, social and economic consequences.

Holt, P.M., Lambton, A.K.S. and Lewis, B., eds, *The Cambridge History of Islam*, vol. 2A, 1970.
The treatment includes the Indian subcontinent, South East Asia and Africa.
Hsu, I.C.Y., *The Rise of Modern China*, 1970.
From 1600, covering traditional institutions, political structures and intellectual trends.
Jansen, M.B., ed., *The Emergence of Meiji Japan*, 1995.
Constitutional rule at home, imperialism abroad.
Jones, M.A., *The Limits of Liberty: American History 1607–1980*, 1983.
Treats the expanding vision, manifest destiny and global involvement.
Mortimer, E., *Faith and Power: the Politics of Islam*, 1982.
The historical background and six twentieth-century case studies.
Seton-Watson, H., *The Russian Empire 1801–1917*, 1988 edn.
Political and social history with emphasis on non-Russian peoples.

VI   Global Tendencies

Wallerstein, I., *The Modern World-System*, vol. 3: *1730–1840*, 1989.
The second era of great expansion of the capitalist world-economy. The incorporation of new zones and the settler decolonization of the Americas.
Harley, C.K., *The Integration of the World Economy, 1850–1914*, 1996.
Increases in population, production and trade, particularly in the United States and Europe, as international trade became global in a multilateral system of payments.
Eichengreen, B., *The Reconstruction of the International Economy, 1945–1960*, 1996.
Postwar boom in trade and lending in the Bretton Woods era.
Coates, D., *Models of Capitalism*, 2000.
Growth and stagnation in the modern era based on the UK, US, Germany and Japan.
Thomson, D., ed., *The Era of Violence, 1858–1945*, 1964, vol. 12 in the New Cambridge Modern History.
Sequence of events in a century of warfare.
Bartlett, C.J., *The Global Conflict*, 1993.
The international rivalry of the great powers, 1880–1990, from the end of the European balance of power to the end of the Cold War.
Seton-Watson, H., *Nations and States*, 1977.
An enquiry into the origins and politics of nationalism on a global scale.
Mazlish, B. and Buultjens, B., eds, *Conceptualising Global History*, 1993.
Theoretical and applied global history, an exploratory study.

Winston, B., *Media Technology and Society*, 1998.
A history from the telegraph to the internet.
Friedman, T., *The Lexus and the Olive Tree*, 1999.
A journalistic account of finance, markets, nation-states, and technology, driving change across the globe.
Held, D., McGrew, A., Goldblatt, D. and Perraton, J., *Global Transformations*, 1999.
Political science, economics and history in a definitive work surveying the globalization debate in an authoritative interdisciplinary study.

Additional sources

Beyer, P., *Religion and Globalisation*, 1994.
The interaction between religion and worldwide social change.
Bracher, K.D., *The Age of Ideologies*, 1998.
A history of political thought in the twentieth century.
Clark, R.P., *The Global Imperative*, 1997.
An interpretive history of the spread of mankind.
Crosby, A.W., *Ecological Imperialism*, 1986.
Traces the predominance of people of European descent in temperate zones of the world, stressing biological rather than military factors.
Diamond, J., *Guns, Germs and Steel*, 1997.
Discusses how the natural world limits and determines the human range of choice.
Gamble, A. and Payne, A., eds, *Regionalism and World Order*, 1996.
Discusses movement towards regional economic blocs, particularly in the Americas, Europe and South East Asia.
Joll, J., *The Origins of the First World War*, 1984.
An analysis of the historical forces at work in the Europe of 1914.
Kennedy, P., *The Rise and Fall of the Great Powers*, 1988.
Economic change and military conflict from the preindustrial to the bipolar world.
Keylor, W.R., *The Twentieth Century World*, 1996.
International relations through the world wars, the Cold War and from 1985 to 1995.
Kindleberger, C.P., *The World in Depression, 1929–1939*, 1986.
The slump and its aftermath.
King, A. and Schneider, B., *The First Global Revolution*, 1991.
Treats of global dimensions beyond the scope of individual governments.
Meadows, D.H., Meadows, D.L., Randers, J. and Behrens, W.W., *The Limits to Growth*, 1972.
The Club of Rome's project on the predicament of mankind.
Milward, A.S., *War, Economy and Society, 1939–1945*, 1977.
The total mobilization of resources in different Allied and Axis countries.

Robertson, E.M., ed., *The Origins of the Second World War*, 1971.
The historians and their materials, a selection of viewpoints.
Van der Wee, H., *Prosperity and Upheaval: the World Economy 1945–1980*, 1987.
The events and the institutional framework.

Index